MILLENNIALS in the WORKPLACE

Also by Dr. Candace Steele Flippin

Generation Z in the Workplace: Helping the Newest Generation in the Workforce Build Successful Working Relationships and Career Paths

MILLENNIALS

in the

WORKPLACE

HELPING THE LARGEST GENERATION GROUP
SUCCEED AT WORK AND IN THEIR CAREERS

DR. CANDACE STEELE FLIPPIN

Library of Congress Control Number: 2017909078

ISBN: 978-0-9986384-6-1
ISBN 978-0-9986384-2-3 (eBook)

Printed in the United States of America
First Edition, 2017

In her second book, *Millennials in the Workplace*, multigenerational workplace scholar Dr. Candace Steele Flippin offers research-based insights and easy-to-follow exercises designed to help the 54 million Millennial (also known as Gen Y) workers build successful career paths and productive relationships with their supervisors.

By distilling her research down into practical tips for Millennials as well as their supervisors, *Millennials in the Workplace* provides a roadmap for a successful career journey and productive workplace environment.

Millennial/Gen Y workers will discover:
- How to communicate and work with other generations
- How to better relate to their supervisor
- Career advice insights from other Millennials
- Tools to create a career development plan

Supervisors of Millennial/Gen Y workers will learn:
- How to help develop Millennial workers
- Key career priorities for Millennials
- What Millennials want from their managers to help them succeed
- The behaviors that limit Millennials at work

DEDICATION

This book is dedicated to Mitchell V. Morse and the generosity of his wife, Beth, who honors his legacy by supporting grateful scholars like me with scholarships to pursue our research passions in his name.

ACKNOWLEDGMENTS

This book follows my bestseller, Generation Z in the Workplace, which was propelled forward by an amazing group of supporters—Thomas, Stacy, T.J., Vicki, Cindy, Janine, Casey, Meaghan, Alison, Carolynn, Gregg, Oral, Monica, Jess, Michael, Don, Hani, Kim, Rodney, Nicole, Hillery, Karen, Geoff, Kelly, and Rachel. I am forever grateful for your support.

I'm appreciative of everyone who helped with the background research, editing, and production of this book. A very special thanks to Elaina, Chad, Lana, Robert, Nicholas, Zachery, Sammy, and Marianna for helping me bring my research to life.

CONTENTS

ABOUT THIS BOOK

According to 2015 U.S. Census numbers, there are 83.1 million Millennials (also referred to as Generation Y) and approximately 54 million are in the workforce. This figure represents over one quarter of the United States population, exceeding 75.4 million Baby Boomers.[1] A Pew Research Center study reports that the numbers of Generation Y in the American workforce have surpassed not only those of the Baby Boomers, but those of Generation X as well.[2]

As the Baby Boomers continue to retire at record rates, their exit from the workforce creates a major opportunity for the younger generations to be more influential in the workplace. There are wide and diverse discussions around how Generation X, Y, and Z leaders are affecting the labor force in the United States, both in vast generalities as well as in particulars, down to industry and or position.

Just as my previous bestselling book, *Generation Z in the Workplace*, took a close look at the Gen Z presence in the workforce, *Millennials in the Workplace* explores insights into the Millennial cohort, based on research findings that examined values, goals, attitudes, and workplace preferences of each of the generations in the labor force today. Some of my research results surprised me, challenging common and frequently negative perceptions about each generation. I used the information I learned from the research to create a resource to help each generation to navigate and attain successful careers. It is my belief that a few insight-driven suggestions, coupled with hard work and personal commitment, can guide Millennials toward achieving the success and the careers they want.

Whether you are reading as a member of the Millennial workforce, a coworker of Millennials, or as a supervisor of Millennial employees, I hope you will read *Millennials in the Workplace* with an open mind and come away optimistic and inspired for the future of the workplace and for the opportunities ahead.

Everyone has something to offer.

INTRODUCTION

While most people will agree that the younger generations are our future, it seems older generations often cast doubt on the behaviors and ability of the younger generations to deliver on the promise of a bright future. The current favorite target: the Millennials. Recent surveys have found that 71% of Americans believe Millennials are a selfish group, while 65% think they have an entitlement problem. Broad generalizations are made every day and in every context about the 83 million Millennials (also referred to as Generation Y).[3]

Public and private opinion about each generational cohort varies greatly from favorable to neutral to negative. Opinion is influenced by media reports along with personal life experiences. In looking at the work of engaging the generations well, many of us are being forced to question what we are hearing and reading about the different generations.

We hear about Millennials on the news regarding ways their attitudes and behaviors are disrupting business. They are featured in comedies. We read about disheartening examples of how economic downturns have burdened them with debt and fewer opportunities. Sometimes, we get glimmers of their accomplishments. Mostly, the conversations are negative or doubtful. However, this book deliberately looks for the best in the Millennial generation, seeking a framework that can help us understand Millennials and help them succeed on the job and in their careers. Given the size of this particular population and the significant ways they are affecting society, we would do ourselves a disservice if we neglected to examine them in finer detail. Every effort at bridging the gap will lead to greater success for us all.

The complex workplace of the 21st century becomes even more challenging with so many different generation groups involved.

Currently, there might be up to five different cohorts employed together in a workplace.

- Traditionalist born 1922–1945
- Baby Boomer born 1946–1964
- Generation X born 1965–1980
- **Generation Y (Millennials) born 1981–1995**
- Generation Z born after 1995

The multigenerational workplace poses real challenges for managers and human resource departments tasked with creating a productive and profitable company. Leadership must be able to accommodate a wide range of tools and practices that each generation prefers and considers indispensable. They must also be aware of and tap into an immense assortment of motivators and behaviors in order to create the workplace culture their workers find agreeable.[4]

When each new generation reaches the workplace, they bring their particular approach to life into their offices, warehouses, storefronts, and jobsites. As the population of the incoming generation increases, their perspectives and values will inevitably run up against the established way of doing things, and it is very likely that there will be conflict. As Gen Y reaches middle and upper management, the results, depending on how generational differences are handled, can have both negative and positive repercussions on the morale and productivity of the department or the company.

Generational-Based Judgment Can Get in the Way of Understanding and Growth

In my first book, *Generation Z in the Workplace,* I noted that while interviewing a young professional and a more seasoned executive as part of my research, the reality struck me that there is always more than one side to any story.

> There are so many negative stereotypes about Millennials and there are so many negative articles on Millennials. It's always in my news feed, you know? Millennials think of this or Millennials need to be better at this. I'll read it but then I normally reassure myself that I'm not doing what they say that the Millennials are bad at doing.
>
> **Gen Y Female**

> I had to remind myself many times in the last couple of decades that I can't be frustrated with my 25-year-old employees for not being 50 years old. I have to allow them to be 25 and allow and acknowledge that there's learning ahead and don't be too harsh on them as they have lessons and foibles and stumbles. Some of these things that they're doing, that we've done now many times over, they're doing for the first time.
>
> **Gen X Male**

Sound familiar? It made me wonder what can be done to help the various generations—Baby Boomers, Gen X, Gen Y (a.k.a. Millennials), and Gen Z—relate to one another better at work. If people tend to act on preconceived notions rather than getting to know each person individually, how does that contribute to conflict and stress in the workplace? Moreover, how can greater awareness of these potential pitfalls help people enrich their careers?

The young woman quoted above acknowledged that her age group has a less than ideal reputation, yet she feels that the stereotypes don't apply to her. Despite her view that she is not a typical Millennial, she still finds herself as a target for those with a bone to pick with her generation. It is clear that negative generalizations are not helpful, can be hurtful, and can impede both team productivity and personal success. Yet they are often tossed around casually, as if they are universally true.

So how can members of the different generations see beyond the stereotypes and instead focus on the positive traits of each cohort to build more unity and cooperation? I embarked on a study to get a sense of what matters to the different generations in life and for their careers. I explored values, how they feel about their time working, and their thoughts on success and their career.

Where do We Go from Here?

The Baby Boomers will have mostly retired from the workplace within the next ten years, and there are simply not enough Gen X members to take their place. Generation Y, now roughly in their early twenties to mid-thirties, are filling the ranks, becoming middle and top managers, and driving a considerable portion of the economy. For better or worse, it is highly likely that more people will be working with and for individuals who are younger than themselves, be they direct supervisors, business partners, customers, or clients.

Who are the much-maligned Millennials? What makes them tick? What aptitudes and challenges do they present in the workplace? We can all be better prepared for this workforce transition by developing a more in-depth understanding of this generation and discovering the best gifts and talents this group brings to the table.

1

WHAT DO WE
KNOW ABOUT MILLENNIALS?

> I have not felt like I was ever so much on a track.
> I think that's been a blessing and a curse. I have set
> goals and I've hit goals that I've set for myself and
> I haven't been completely meandering. But I've never
> felt necessarily like all of the pieces were snapping
> into place.
>
> **Gen Y Male**

> There are so many negative stereotypes about
> Millennials and there are so many negative articles
> on Millennials. It's always in my news feed, you know?
> Millennials think of this or Millennials need to be better
> at this. I'll read it but then I normally reassure myself
> that I'm not doing what they say that the Millennials are
> bad at doing.
>
> **Gen Y Female**

Why Is This Generation Called "Millennial" and "Gen Y"?

Where did the title "Millennial" originate? In 1991, generational historians Neil Howe and William Strauss examined American history through a series of biographies that took a close look at the collections of traits that they detected in common across each generation group associated with 20-year time spans. At the time that they started their work, generational studies were not common. Naming the Baby Boomers was easy, but the following generation, Generation X, didn't get a "real" name. However, Howe explained that they chose "Millennial" for the next generation because they would begin graduating high school in the year 2000. The year 2000 offered promises of both threat and prosperity, and the generation entering adulthood at the century mark was seen by older generations as similarly unpredictable.[5]

Use of the moniker "Generation Y" or "Gen Y" naturally followed use of "Generation X." Given the closeness in the associated birth years in the literature, Millennial and Gen Y are used synonymously in this book.

The name Millennial stuck after a 2013 Time magazine article entitled "The Me Me Me Generation" covered the cohort in critical and dismissive terms. Google Trends, an online search volume tracker, showed a spike in usage of the term Millennial to refer to this generation from that point. Most members of Generation Y have found the moniker derogatory.[6] Certainly, there seems to be a great deal of negative connotation attached to the term "Millennial" in the minds of many. One can just search for "Millennial" online and find headline after headline that paints this generation in negative light. In some regards, those in this generation face unfair prejudice simply because of widespread and undeserved stereotypes associated with the name.

Snapshot of the Millennial Generation

The Millennials were born roughly between 1981 and 1995, aged 21 to 35 at the time of my study. Here I explore an overview of what shapes their perspectives.

Technology can be considered a symbol of identity for Millennials. Gen Y uses all types of internet and cell phone technology much more than the older generations, for such daily activities as staying in touch with friends and family, attending college and work meetings, shopping, banking and investing, producing creative work, playing games, and watching movies and TV.

Seventy-four percent of Millennials said they felt that new technology makes life easier. Fifty-four percent said it makes people closer to family and friends. Fifty-two percent saw new technology as a way to use their time more efficiently.[7]

Connection to family is central to the Millennial sense of well-being. Millennials' parents tended to be very engaged with their kids, even while divorcing, and Generation Y continues with this family-centered focus. While 59% of Millennials in a 2014 Gallup poll were single or never married, the same survey indicates that they expect to marry and to have children. Nearly half of single, 34-year-old Millennials have children. Nine percent of Millennials are in domestic partnership living arrangements, and 36% are in multi-adult households of three or more.[8]

Perhaps some of these family arrangements are by financial necessity, even so they also reflect the way Millennials are rearranging societal patterns at large. They are delaying marriage and cohabiting as ways to avoid divorce, which many experienced in their own families or witnessed in the families of their friends. Additionally, Millennials are more likely than the older generations to create households with LGBT partners, and until very recently, many of these arrangements have not fallen into any family category typically included in polls.[9]

Many Millennials have immigrant parents or are immigrants themselves, which has made the generation more ethnically diverse and tolerant than older generations. For Gen Y, gender and race are seen as simply reflecting distinctive experiences and an array of opinions to be assimilated and respected, instead of being associated with hiring or school enrollment quotas. In most cases, they have not had to think twice about schoolmates and work colleagues who speak different languages and wear different clothing and observe different religious and cultural practices as a matter of daily public life.

The Millennials have also been shaped by:

Man-made disasters: Environmental impacts such as the Exxon Valdez oil spill and the Chernobyl nuclear accident.

War: The start of the Gulf War in 1990 and the United States military involvement in the Middle East ever since.

Violence: The erosion of the perception of the general safety of the world with airline bombings such as Pan Am Flight 103 over Lockerbie, Scotland, school shootings like Columbine and Virginia Tech, the Oklahoma City bombing, and the events of 9/11.

Marriage equality: The first issuance of same-sex marriage licenses in Massachusetts in 2004 and the legalization of same-sex marriages across the land in 2015.

President Obama: Election of the United States' first African-American president in 2008.

Economic downturns: The real-time and deeply personal household impacts of the housing bubble bust and the Great Recession that began in 2007, and the continuing burden of high student debt and under-employment.[10]

Looking Ahead with Millennials

In spite of the previous experiences, Millennials are well on their way along their chosen path and in the process of finding out the particular changes they are making in their world. What trends in society will they be facing going forward?

TRENDS IN THE WORKPLACE

Technology. The workplace is fully technology driven by the Millennials' arrival. The instant exchange of information over virtually any distance has made it possible for companies to operate seamlessly regardless of whether the principal players are abroad or at home. Computer science and information technology careers have grown exponentially as more and more companies seek technology solutions to keep up with the future.[11]

These technology trends have facilitated the rise of the on-demand economy, in which workers can provide services to employers on a case-by-case basis, over great distances, and without the need for formal hiring and on-boarding. Over one-third of Millennials are independent workers, whether by choice (preferring the arrangement to the traditional 9-5) or by need (taking gigs on the side to make ends meet).

Some 32% of Generation Y see themselves in flexible working arrangements in the coming years.[12] Self-employment options with companies such as Lyft and Airbnb offer additional income opportunities that are within an individual's control.

Employment shifts. Looking at the workplace overall, permanent, part-time, and temporary hiring is on the rise in 2017, and wages are rising as well. Employers are putting increased emphasis on employee "soft skills" like positive attitude, reliability, and ability to work on a team.[13]

Seventy-five million Baby Boomers are retiring and 65 million Gen X workers will not be sufficient to take their place. The Millennials will be challenged to fill the remaining education, management, and skills gap.[14]

Work preferences. Millennials are technology multitaskers who see themselves as working smarter, not being lazy, when they prefer to draft communications while on the train and craft the finer points of their proposals in the café down the street. They prefer to *work to live* rather than *live to work,* and combine creative and income endeavors into their social life. Often, these attitudes put them at odds with employers with traditional frameworks and expectations. Additionally, Millennials tend to prefer constant positive feedback, and if they don't feel valued and satisfied in their job arrangements, they will network themselves right into another job.[15]

TRENDS IN CULTURE

Generation Y is currently adapting to and influencing a wide variety of societal changes that are taking shape over the next few decades.

Life in the cloud. By 2020, there will be approximately 5 billion internet users on 80 billion devices worldwide. This connectivity will encompass work, home, and surrounding environments, turning them into a "seamless experience." Our lifestyle preferences will dwell in the cloud and travel with us as we navigate the offline world. "Smart" (connected, customizable, sensing, and self-monitoring) services, solutions, and governance will be the normal way of life.[16]

Sustainability. Innovators will come closer to developing cars with zero emissions or accidents, cities with zero carbon footprints, and factories with minimal environmental impact. Whether this will become reality, more and more studies indicate that Millennials want and will pay more for products that support sustainability, made by companies that tangibly support positive environmental and social impact.[17]

Affordable living. Millennials watched up close and personal as the real estate collapse led family and friends and neighbors into foreclosure, and the experience has colored their enthusiasm for home ownership. They do not feel, as the older generations did, that owning a home is necessarily part of the path to wealth accumulation, although for the most part, they see themselves owning a home eventually.[18] For now, they live with parents or rent, sharing housing with family or others and finding smaller quarters they can responsibly afford. In line with modest housing needs, many Millennials like to be near friends, work, services, and leisure locations, and some prefer walking and biking over owning a car.[19]

The evolving definition of success. Along with their housing choices, Generation Y is making other statements that run contrary to the long-held views of Baby Boomers and Generation X. Many Millennials do not measure their success by dollars earned. They do want a fair salary, yet many are preferring to earn less at something they love to do rather than earn more at something they dislike, they find it more important to achieve personal goals and make a positive difference in their community.[20]

Embracing diversity and equality. Generation Y was born during a time of increased immigration and decreasing Caucasian birth rates.

Thus, they span a demographic gap between older, "whiter" generations and the racial and ethnic diversity of coming Gen Z and younger generations. They make up 23% of the total U.S. population; 27% of the total minority population are Gen Y. Millennials comprise 30% of the voting age population, and 38% of the total voting age of minority voters. Thirty-eight percent of the workforce are Millennials, and Millennial minorities make up 43% of the total working age population.[21]

In the 18–34 Millennial age bracket, 55.8% are Caucasian. Diversity is broadening as Asians, Hispanics, and those who identify as two or more races comprise nearly 30% of the Gen Y population in the U.S., and African Americans account for about 14%. This generation's passion for advocacy and tolerance will be key in leading the nation to more successful racial diversity policies.[22]

Diversity for Gen Y is broader than race or ethnicity. Equality is a major concern, whether it's racial, sexual, educational, religious, economic, or otherwise. Many of these issues are being addressed in the higher courts, and the rulings are having widespread implications on the community, culture, business, and even on the personal level. Millennials feel that many aspects of our society are broken, and their active participation in politics will be key to healing much of what they see as disappointing.

Political influence. In 2008, Barack Obama won Millennial voters—18-to 29-year-olds—by 34 points. The voters also turned out in high numbers, comprising about 18% of the electorate.[23] Preferring not to be labeled and associated with a political party, nearly 60% of Millennials claimed to be independent, many identified with Bernie Sanders, an avowed independent and Democrat, and with Donald Trump, an outsider business leader with no political experience and few ties to the GOP establishment. Having observed many corporate and political scandals, this generation wary of government and large institutions had an affinity for a candidate who they perceived as representing change and as credible in terms of how they presented their true selves.[24] The impact of the Millennials as a voting populace, coupled with high unemployment among Millennials in certain parts of the U.S.

and narrow margins of support for Hillary Clinton in a number of key population segments,[25] led a number of analysts to point to the Millennials as a significant contributor to the results of 2016 election cycle. The long and short of it is that Gen Y has the numbers to create the change they want.

Given the generation's large size, insistence on accountability, and changing values, Millennials are set to play a significant role in shaping the changing face of society. This likely includes the policies that affect our workplaces, environment, communities, and daily lives.

■ ■ ■

Millennials in the Workplace

The following chapters look at a few specific characteristics of Generation Y. Each section will conclude with practical tips for Millennial workers as they navigate challenges and opportunities in their careers, and for managers of Gen Y workers. Let's look more closely at Millennial values, goals, workplace preferences, and attitudes.

2
VALUES

> I think there are some weeks where if I know my week is pretty hectic from a work perspective, then the balance may lean towards more of a 75% to 25%, work to free-time. Annually, ideally most of my time is more driven by work. I would say it's more of a 70% work to 30% free-time.
>
> **Gen Y Female**

> I think that so much could be accomplished if people just worked together in a way that was respectful. I think that a lot more could be accomplished if we peeled back a few layers and forced people to work together more.
>
> **Gen Y Female**

Values are principles or standards of behavior that one holds to be important. Our values, generally framed by societal norms,[26] shape the way we think about what's going on in the world, the words we use to express ourselves, and the ways we act in different circumstances. When we make decisions, we are influenced in one direction or another by our values.

What Does Gen Y Value?

Professional and personal values shape our priorities and how we manifest them in our private lives and at work. In this chapter, we take a look at what Gen Y values. As this generational cohort has become the largest in the workforce and begins to take on more and more management positions, their values will have a greater and greater impact on the workplace and eventually on society as a whole.

Two fundamental topics examined in my study were personal and professional values. In order to understand what motivates individuals, it is helpful to understand what they want out of life and the work- or career-related pursuits toward which they will direct their energy.

Overview of Gen Y Personal Values

Starting with personal values, the survey participants were asked *What is most important to you in your life right now from a personal perspective?*

Gen Y Ranking for Personal Values in Order of Importance
1. Relationships (*e.g.,* family, friends, *etc.*)
2. Happiness
3. Health
4. Financial Security
5. Career
6. Faith

For Gen Y, *relationships* was ranked first as the most important to the respondents as a group, followed by *happiness, health, financial security, career,* and *faith.*

In my study, Gen Y ranks both *happiness* and *faith* significantly higher than do any of the other three cohorts. Not surprisingly, given the stark realities of the economic downturn of the past decade, *financial security* is equally important for all the generation groups.

One matter of some interest is the relatively high ranking of *health,* even over *financial security* and *career.* Millennials, unlike older generations, view health and wellness as many small actions taken as part of their daily routines rather than a compartmentalized segment consisting of conventional medical practices. They agree with the other generations on the basic priorities for health and wellness, like getting enough sleep, exercise, and water, but less than half of Millennials are likely to plan ahead with regularly scheduled checkups, vaccinations, preventive screenings, or obtaining health insurance. Instead, they are more inclined to pursue alternative medical practices such as natural, organic, and non-toxic food sources, relaxation and unplugging from technology, and maintaining healthy relationships.[27]

When the Millennials rank their personal values, both men and women agree that *relationships* and *happiness* are most important. Gen Y Men and women rank *relationships* highest among the choices offered.

Gen Y Ranking for Personal Values in Order of Importance	
MEN	WOMEN
1. Relationships	1. Relationships
2. Happiness	2. Happiness
3. Health	3. Health
4. Financial Security	4. Financial Security
5. Career	5. Career
6. Faith	6. Faith

Overview of Gen Y Professional Values

Regarding professional values, I asked **What is important to you professionally right now?**

The Gen Y respondents ranked the following six value concepts in order of importance: *making more money, doing well in current role, work/life balance, promotion, changing career, and retirement.*

Gen Y Ranking for Professional Values in Order of Importance
1. Making More Money
2. Doing Well in Current Role
3. Work/life Balance
4. Promotion
5. Changing Career
6. Retirement

Gen Y entered the workforce approximately 18 years ago and many may be on their third or fourth job. Their values and expectations have been influencing the workplace for nearly two decades. The participants in my study had job tenures that ranged from over 10 years with the same employer (19%), six to 10 years (20%), three to five years (19%), one to two years (25%), and less than one year (17%).

Gen Y members acknowledge the importance of financial security and value the satisfaction of a job well done, but they are unwilling to sacrifice a personal life on the altar of career success. The finding that Millennials prefer making more money is supported by extensive research in the Deloitte Millennial Survey, which states that pay and benefits are the most important deciding factors for Millennials choosing an employer. In addition, many are facing life stage changes related to starting families and the associated financial needs. However, with compensation being taken out of the picture, the next most important deciding factor is ability to create and maintain a work/life balance.[28]

The Millennial emphasis on personal relationships and happiness highlighted in the discussion on personal values would certainly reflect a prioritization of social values over material gain. It is likely that experiencing and observing financial hardships while growing up cemented a deep need in Gen Y to never be put into financial straits again, while at the same time driving home the reality that money troubles can lead to considerable disruption of important relationships.

Along these lines, the popular press notes that Millennials invest in personal relationships in the workplace much more than do Gen X and the Baby Boomers.[29] Other reports on Gen Y show greater work satisfaction when they feel they have emotional support and friendship through their working hours.[30]

In contrast to popular opinion about Millennials and their money habits related to spending and saving, Generation Y actually puts away a greater percentage of their paychecks than other generations.[31] They are quite careful about how they spend, and do what they can to cut expenses using such strategies as getting roommates, delaying home purchases, tracking spending with smart phone apps, and budgeting smaller amounts for activities than other generations are used to budgeting. Lower-paying jobs and financial hardships during formative years have made these habits a necessity. Saving for retirement is a considerable priority for Gen Y, compared to other groups of American earners.[32]

It is important to note some gender nuances. As in the ranking of personal values, men and women shared similar professional values, only reversing the order of the top two. Men ranked *making more money* first and women ranked *doing well in the current role* first. When thinking about development planning, Millennial supervisors should keep in mind that this generation wants to perform well in their current role and they expect to be compensated and financially rewarded for their performance.

Gen Y Ranking for Professional Values in Order of Importance by Gender	
MEN	WOMEN
1. Making More Money	1. Doing Well in Role
2. Doing Well in Role	2. Making More Money
3. Work/life Balance	3. Work/life Balance
4. Getting a Promotion	4. Getting a Promotion
5. Changing Career	5. Changing Career
6. Retirement	6. Retirement

Gen Y and the American Dream

> My parents come from a low economic background and because of sheer hard work they pretty much made themselves a middle class family. I feel like those lessons and those values that I learned allow me to transition into my own – I was able to establish and find my own job. I'm also starting at the middle class as well. I feel like I can only go up from there. I have to just stay the course and stay on that plan. It's gotten me this far and I feel like it will get me even further in the future.
>
> **Gen Y Male**

> I'm a hard worker. I enjoy working and I can't imagine ever not doing something. But I work a lot now and I look forward to a time when I don't have to work as much and spend much more time with my family and we can travel, etc. Until then, not having to worry about affording everything that I would like to do would be the American dream.
>
> **Gen Y Male**

In *Generation Z in the Workplace,* I first explored values in the context of one's expectations by generation group based on efforts made and potential rewards gained. This concept is important to the values discussion for U.S. citizens and is often associated with the concept of the *American Dream*. This ideal was famously described by James Truslow Adams in 1931, who stated that "life should be better and richer and fuller for everyone, with opportunity for each according to ability or achievement," not impeded by social rank, circumstances of birth, or other similar barriers.[33] The American Dream as an ideal is widely reported on in the popular press and was a key topic among candidates in the last U.S. election. I continue my exploration of this concept for Gen Y to provide perspective on their expectations.

Pursuit of education and home ownership have generally been seen as the benchmarks of the American Dream, while different generations and different economic trends have squeezed other facets into or out of the broader understanding of the concept over the years. As a national ethos, it implies the virtues and rewards of hard work and determination.

Many Americans have expressed concern that the traditional American Dream may no longer be representative of what the average American can truly attain. By and large, they point to the economic reality that many households have trouble just paying the bills on a monthly basis, and have no possibility of saving for higher education or buying a house. Other people have sought to adjust their concept of the American Dream to encompass personal fulfillment and attainment of their own set of ideals.

To better understand Gen Y's perceptions of the American Dream, I asked the study participants to rank six concepts based on how important they are to their version of the American Dream. They ranked the concepts in this order: *being able to achieve goals, financial security, ability to pursue education, freedom of speech, home ownership, and building a legacy.*

Gen Y Ranking for the American Dream in Order of Importance
1. Ability to Achieve Goals
2. Financial Security
3. Ability to Pursue Education
4. Freedom of Speech
5. Home Ownership
6. Building a Legacy

When the members of Gen Y were asked if they believe that their version of the American Dream is achievable, an overwhelming 88% said YES! This response is lower than Gen Z (95%) but still higher than Gen X (83%) or Baby Boomers (80%). I consider this high percentage encouraging, given the dramatic events that have shaped their lives to date. Overall, 87% of Americans in my study still believe the American Dream is achievable.

It is hard to find a job that will pay what is needed to achieve the American Dream and have job security to keep that job.

Gen Y Female

I am a single mother. I have a job, but my income is not enough for me to live on.

Gen Y Female

Gen Y male and female respondents, when examined separately, expressed completely different priorities for their vision of the elements of the American Dream. *Being able to achieve goals* and *financial security* were at the top for both, although males valued achievement of *goals* over *financial security*, and the females vice versa. *Home ownership* and *building a legacy* ranked at the bottom of the list, which is not surprising, having already noted that Millennials are delaying home ownership in favor of lower expenses and higher savings.

| Gen Y Ranking for Professional Values in Order of Importance by Gender ||
MEN	WOMEN
1. Ability to Achieve Goals	1. Financial Security
2. Financial Security	2. Ability to Achieve Goals
3. Freedom of Speech	3. Ability to Pursue Education
4. Ability to Pursue Education	4. Freedom of Speech
5. Building a Legacy	5. Home Ownership
6. Home Ownership	6. Building a Legacy

As shown in the table above, males chose this order: *being able to achieve goals, financial security, freedom of speech, ability to pursue education, building a legacy, home ownership*. The females selected this order: *financial security, being able to achieve goals, ability to pursue an education, freedom of speech, home ownership, building a legacy*.

Twelve percent of the Gen Y participants indicated that they felt the American Dream was not achievable. I asked them to share a reason. Financial reasons were the primary factors that seemed to limit access to the American Dream for this generational cohort. For 84%, lack of money was the primary reason they felt the American Dream was not real for them. Debt, low wages, and generally dismal economic realities were cited as other factors that made the American Dream seem unavailable.

While finances are a challenge for some, on the whole, most Millennials are optimistic and firmly aware of the fact that their financial success is up to them. In response to the financial difficulties experienced growing up, they practice, what some may consider, frugality as an everyday habit. Even as such, they value personal connections and happiness more than the almighty dollar, preferring success on their own terms over the more predictable paths followed by their elders.

It should be noted that a recent survey of the general population found that roughly half of Millennials think that the American dream is "dead."[34] The difference between my survey and the general population survey is that my respondents are all employed, while general population surveys include full-time employment, part-time employment, under- or unemployment, and non-employment. This distinction provides important context—my book is aimed at the working population and reflects those perspectives.

Additionally, in other general population surveys, among Millennials who had a college degree, nearly 60% agreed that the American Dream was attainable.[35] Thirty-one percent of my survey respondents had some amount of college education including an Associate's degree; 52% had a completed a Bachelor's degree or higher. This higher proportion of college-educated respondents would account for the much higher than average percentage of general population Millennials who believe the American Dream is attainable.

Implications for Work Success and Career Paths

Job satisfaction, compensation, and great performance generally come down to how expectations and hopes match up with day-to-day realities: whether you can accomplish what is required on something close enough to your own terms that you don't experience a great deal of frustration. When working across generations, sometimes the smallest differences in thinking and priority levels can lead to the largest misunderstandings and conflicts. Gen Y values boil down to the fact that they want to have a salary that allows them to meet their current and future needs without too much disruption of their ability to be successful in their personal lives. Furthermore, they also want to do well on the job and to advance in their career. Open exploration of these priorities can forestall a great deal of tension in workplace discussions.

■ ■ ■

Consider the following statements:

"All my life, I've always done well and received positive feedback about all my efforts, even when things didn't turn out great. I got praise for my efforts. In the past three months, I've taken on more tasks and even inconvenienced myself. Why doesn't my boss take my request for a raise or promotion seriously?" – Gen Y Female

"When I started my career, I had to really pay my dues with long hours, taking on "growth" assignments and performing the "other duties assigned" more than I can count. I've mainly had on-review cycle promotions. She is a great worker with lots of promise but I just don't get how someone thinks that taking on a few extra assignments for a few weeks means they now deserve a raise and promotion. I'm giving her more to help round out her skills for the current job and set her up for future roles. Perhaps, I should pick someone else..." – Gen X Female

It's clear that both of these individuals believe that promotion should be based on merit, but both have different opinions about what merit really is. In this case, it would be helpful if they could have a candid conversation about their individual experiences and expectations, and what the issue looks like to each individual involved. Open-minded and honest communication is generally the best way to come to an understanding and forge agreements about priorities and progress.

Practical Suggestions for Millennial/Gen Y Employees

No matter what sector you work in, competition for resources, customers, and talent is challenging. Many employers are struggling to adopt and adapt to the ways that Gen Y values and expectations are changing the workplace. Managers are balancing the goals of the organization against the need to drive performance while keeping their teams intact. Your needs may be competing with many organizational priorities.

❒ **Stay true to your values, but make sure you and your manager are aligned.** You value your employer, want to work hard and have time for the things that matter most to you outside of your job. It is important that you ensure that you and your boss are on the same page about your work style, habits, and need for your own time.

❒ **Be patient.** It can be frustrating to feel that you always have to explain or justify yourself—especially when you believe the answers are clear from your point of view. Perhaps your supervisor has different values than you have. Find neutral ways to express your own perspective so others know where you're coming from. Instead of becoming defensive, respond with statements that show the benefits of your ideas in terms of what your manager or co-workers value.

❒ **Make sure you and your manager are aligned on what hard word looks like.** While you may be committed to working hard and are prepared to put yourself into the best position for receiving raises and promotions, your supervisor or your supervisor's boss may have a different perspective. Your most important values should guide your decisions, but finding out what your supervisors expect is equally important.

Questions to Ask Your Supervisor

What does success look like in this role?

- How will my performance be measured?
- How am I doing in my role?
- What does "above and beyond" look like?
- Who weighs in on the decision to award raises and promotions?

What is my next step?

- In my current role?
- What do you see as my areas for development?

Exercise 1
Preparing for Success

List the questions you will ask your supervisor about what success in your current role looks like and how you can best position yourself for raises and promotions.

1.

2.

3.

Who can you practice with to help you have a productive conversation?

- Mentor?
- Parent?
- Friend?

Practical Suggestions for Supervisors of Millennials/Gen Y

Your Millennial employee likely is entertaining the same aspirations that you once had. Some are just beginning their careers, others are mid-career, and all want to know how to position themselves for the next step. Knowing what you know now, what would you tell your younger self about success and, more importantly, how can you share this information to develop your employees?

- ❐ **Set them up for success.** Perhaps when you started your career, the expectations for employees were different than they are today. You might have entered the workplace with an in-depth training program or you might have been left to problem-solve on your own. Surviving a *trial by fire* experience isn't necessarily a badge of honor for Millennials. If they are frustrated and can't see a path toward sustained success, they may leave.

- ❐ **Encourage the practical aspects of career advancement and put the plan in place.** Due to the economy, many Millennials have had a delayed start to their careers and are now eager to catch up. Think of ways to reinforce good work habits and skills that will serve them well in any undertaking, not just in your department. Millennials have several years under their belt and have expectations about growing in their roles and careers.

- ❐ **Be transparent about compensation.** Financial security is important to your Millennial employee, and so they may be focused on advancement and bonuses. It will be important to have conversations about compensation in all forms (e.g., salary, bonuses, vacation, other benefits) to manage their expectations.

- ❐ **Recognize how they may be shaped by key personal and professional values.** From a personal perspective, *happiness* and *relationships* ranked highly for Gen Y. Professionally, Gen Y values *making more money* and *doing well in their current role.* As you think about the team atmosphere and your leadership style, consider how the quality of your interactions and the work experience will matter to your Millennial employees. Coaching them to excel on the job and being clear about their opportunities to earn more money will be key to retention.

3

GOALS

> Twenty years from now, I would love to work for a large company in more of a director, vice president role. That's where I could definitely see myself going.
>
> **Gen Y Female**

> I've had the same average pay for ten years now, have changed jobs trying to get ahead with little luck and a lot of frustration.
>
> **Gen Y Female**

What do Millennials want career-wise when they look ahead with long-term goals in mind? Where do they feel they are in relation to where they eventually want to be in their careers, and what informs their choices?

Four major factors influence the lens through which Millennials view their goals and possibilities: possessing higher education, lower relative pay, student loan debt and un- or under-employment. These factors impact Millennial expectations for their career pursuits.

Seeking to prepare themselves for a bright and limitless future, Millennials went to college in droves. In addition, employers need a more educated and highly skilled workforce and, depending on the industry, are reluctant to hire anyone without a diploma in their field. However, Gen Y graduated to find few jobs available, degree or not. Many are unable to find work at all: 8% of 18- to 29-year-olds were unemployed in 2016, compared to 3.7% of the general American population. Many others have been forced to take low-paying and part-time jobs for which they are over-educated.[36]

Millennials who are fortunate enough to have found full-time work have coped with stagnant pay, receiving just a 6% raise from 2007 to 2014, compared to 15% for the senior generational cohorts during the same seven-year timeframe.[37]

How Does Gen Y Feel about Their Career Opportunities?

As part of my research, I asked the Gen Y respondents two questions and gave them the opportunity to explain their answers. The first question: *How do you rate your current career opportunities?* The rating options were *excellent, good, average, poor, and awful.*

The majority of the respondents had favorable views of their career options. Seventy percent of Gen Y rate their career opportunities as *good* or better than good. For a breakdown, 27% of Gen Y rate their career opportunities as *excellent* and 43% rate their career opportunities as *good*. On the whole, Millennial males are more optimistic than are their female counterparts about future career opportunities.

Career Opportunity for Gen Y	
Excellent	27%
Good	43%
Average	23%
Poor	5%
Awful	2%

Even with the delayed start, Gen Y is optimistic about career opportunities:

- 27% of Gen Y are expecting *excellent* opportunities
- 70% of the Gen Y participants (80% of males and 62% of females) rated their career opportunities as *good* or *excellent*
- 28% of Gen Y males rated their career opportunities as *excellent*

- 26% of Gen Y females thought their career prospects were *excellent*

Career Opportunity for Gen Y, by Gender		
	Men	Women
Excellent	28%	26%
Good	51%	36%
Average	19%	26%
Poor	2%	9%
Awful	0%	4%

Twenty-eight percent of Gen Y males rate their career opportunities as *excellent* and 51% rate their career opportunities as *good*. In the study, 80% of Gen Y males rate their career opportunities as *good* or better than good.

Twenty-six percent of Gen Y Females rate their career opportunities as *excellent* and 36% rate their career opportunities as *good*. Sixty-two percent of Gen Y Females rate their career opportunities as *good* or better than good.

What Makes Career Options Excellent for Gen Y?

After receiving their answers about career prospects, I invited the respondents to explain why they answered the way they did. The most common reason cited for an *excellent* career outlook was that they love their job (25%). The next most popular response was a comment related to overall satisfaction with their life (14%). These two kinds of response account for half of the replies. The open-ended responses are listed below.

- *Love my job*
- *Just love everything about my job*
- *I love my life*

- *Things have never looked better*
- *It's everything I want, can't ask for more*
- *I have a lot of career choices*
- *I have a great job*
- *I have a great job with room for growth and I plan to finish college to open up even more opportunities*
- *I am a teacher and I love where I work*
- *I am doing very well and making what I want*
- *I have no complaints*
- *Because I'm happy*
- *Getting better*
- *It's the best job I could ever ask for*
- *Because my financial situation is great*
- *Everything is excellent and so is my career*
- *Because I am having a good time*
- *I am truly loving where my career is taking me*

Seeing many opportunities ahead (14%), receiving good pay (9%), and noting the results of their own focus and hard work (9%) were the next most common reasons cited for an excellent career outlook. Two reasons were given for an *awful* career outlook, the first being scarcity of open positions, the second being no growth in the chosen industry.

Enjoying one's vocation as well as life in general matters to Millennials. These responses are in line with the perception that Millennials place high value on overall life happiness and making sufficient money for their purposes. Doing well in their current role is an important aspect of the work-life balance equation because these finding suggest that fulfillment from and at work is important to Gen Y.

Twenty-three percent of respondents said that their career outlook was *average*, and 7% indicated that their career outlook was *poor* or *awful*. The reasons cited above for awful prospects reflect the reality that the economy has not recovered completely for everyone. Millennials remain optimistic when their situations are perceived as good, but financial realities temper enthusiasm when there is difficulty making ends meet.

Are Millennials on Track for Their Job Goals?

The next question I asked the study participants was *Are you in your ideal job for this stage in your life?* The answers to choose from were *definitely not, probably not, maybe, probably yes,* and *definitely yes.*

Ideal Job for Gen Y	
Definitely Yes	25%
Probably Yes	36%
Maybe	14%
Probably Not	17%
Definitely Not	8%

Twenty-five percent of Gen Y respondents say they are definitely in their ideal job and 36% of Gen Y say they are *probably* in their ideal job. Sixty-one percent of Gen Y say they are *definitely* or *probably* in their ideal job.

Roughly the same proportions who indicated *definitely yes* and *probably yes* (61%) as to whether they were in the ideal job for the current stage in their lives also selected *excellent* and *good* for their career prospects (70%). Viewed in conjunction with numbers in the career outlook section above, job satisfaction is positively correlated to career outlook. It would seem that those Millennials who are able to find good jobs tend to like them very much and see their careers as being on the right track.

The male and female survey participants responded with roughly similar numbers regarding what they thought of their career opportunities. Sixty-four percent of men and 58% of women thought they were *definitely* or *probably* in their ideal jobs; 22% of males and 28% of females reported that they were *definitely* in their ideal jobs.

Ideal Job for Gen Y by Gender		
	Men	Women
Definitely Yes	22%	28%
Probably Yes	42%	30%
Maybe	15%	14%
Probably Not	19%	16%
Definitely Not	2%	12%

The majority of Gen Y males and females tended to feel that they were on track.

- 22% of Gen Y males say they are *definitely* in their ideal job and 42% of Gen Y males say they are *probably* in their ideal job
- 28% of Gen Y females say they are *definitely* in their ideal job and 30% of Gen Y females say they are *probably* in their ideal job
- 64% of Gen Y males say they are *definitely* or *probably* in their ideal job
- 58% of Gen Y females say they are *definitely* or *probably* in their ideal job

I invited the 8% of respondents who said they were *definitely not* in their ideal job to give a reason why. The responses are quite telling. Listed in order of how frequently they were given, the reasons are as follows:

- **In wrong role.** General dissatisfaction with the current position (one-third of those who knew they definitely weren't where they needed to be)
- **Weren't using their training.** That they were in work that did not require the degree they possessed (one-fourth of the those who knew they definitely weren't where they needed to be)
- **Low pay.** They felt under compensated.

- **High stress.** Their job or work environments were too stressful.
- **Lack of advancement.** No room for promotion at current job
- **Settling for what they job they could get.** Nowhere else was hiring

Interestingly, two positive answers showed up among the *definitely not* responses.

- *I want to own my own business*
- *Don't enjoy current work, thinking about a new career*

These individuals are aware that they are ultimately in control of their futures and are able to deal with job dissatisfaction in terms of personal responsibility and working to attain something better. This mindset supports the notion that Millennials tend to reject what doesn't work for them and do what they have to do to get ahead on their own terms.

Implications for Work Success and Career Paths

Many members of Generation Y came out of high school and college to find less than they were promised in terms of access to jobs and promising career tracks. Yet, for the most part, they possess the determination to get out of any rut they may find themselves in. If they have found a good working situation, they want to stay, and many have the pragmatism to rethink their path if they don't see success where they are.

■ ■ ■

Consider the following statements:
"I overheard the department heads last month complaining that the corporate office froze raises and hiring and promotions for the next six months, after my manager said I was definitely due for a raise and consideration for the team

lead. Everyone wonders why I've been so depressed lately. I need the money and I was really hoping for the team lead perks. I used to love it here and I can hardly drag myself in these days. I feel stuck." – Gen Y Male

"You know, I feel like I need a fresh infusion into my career, but I don't know what it's going to be. Maybe I should go look at another company." – Gen Y Female

"I can't believe my ears. One of my managers is concerned that his team isn't happy. Perhaps they would be happier if they were unemployed. I know things are rough, but we aren't making our numbers this quarter. They just have to suck it up." – Baby Boomer Male

"I just took a management position at a new company, only to find out that the person I'm replacing was let go because she lost half her staff inside a year. Now I'm freaked out. How in the world can I be held responsible for people who just decide it's time to leave?" – Gen X Female

■ ■ ■

More and more research is pointing to the idea that happiness at work is no longer just the byproduct of good performance, good pay and perks, and advancement opportunities. Rather, satisfaction with work and meaningful bonds with work colleagues are becoming important factors in successful engagement with job and career. An examination of an extensive collection of studies supports the notion that a high level of personal happiness is related to positive impacts in many areas of life, such as mental and physical health, relationships, income, and social or community involvement.[38]

For the Millennial employee who can articulate her true desires for the workplace, and for the Millennial supervisor who understands that his employees really do have reasons other than capriciousness for leaving their jobs, beneficial conversations can be started around what's important in terms of what it takes to stay and invest in the company. Situations that look one way to one party may look completely different to other parties.

Millennials are realists who know how to cope with less than ideal circumstances if they have some measure of control. They disconnect. They leave. And, they post their experiences on social channels for the entire world to see (and judge your organization). Supervisor transparency can go a long way toward aligning Millennial workers' expectations, and gaining their support and cooperation.

Even if things are great, there may be ways to make things better. If business is uncertain, silence from management can have an unwelcomed effect on employees. Bringing everyone to the table to problem-solve or offer recommendations can help manage expectations and make work environments more inclusive. New ideas can revolutionize departments and companies when employees and supervisors alike are invited to be open and discuss what they would like to see happen. And if solutions are not immediately available, being honest about the situation can also be helpful, as to avoid employees thinking that you are hiding the truth from them.

Practical Suggestions for Millennial/Gen Y Employees

Careers are marathons, not sprints. They require training, hard work, and investment on your part. You will need to be patient sometimes as the needs of the company and the opportunities for advancement and salary increases may not always line up with your expectations. However, you can set yourself up well.

- ❐ **Focus on doing the best job you can in your current role.** Your career plan may be centered on having short stents in a role. Once you feel you have mastered it, you are ready and expect to move up into the next challenge. Some companies do have fast-moving career tracks and tap or move talent outside of scheduled performance cycles. However, most organizations have annual or biannual time frames when promotions or raises can be considered. The key is to perform well in your role and perhaps even over-perform so that you are a better candidate when the opportunity arises. Doing so will also set you up for success in your next role.

- ❐ **Broaden your skill set.** Explore ways you can add value by seeking to gain new skills and work experiences. Consider applying for jobs at the same title or grade level to learn a new skill set or industry, if moving up isn't an option. Identify classes you can take to broaden your knowledge and sharpen your skill sets to make yourself more valuable to your employers and team.

- ❐ **Get ready for leadership.** Perhaps you are years away from managing people. Maybe it's your next step. Or, being a supervisor may not even be on your career radar screen. In any case, the reality is that as Baby Boomers continue to leave the workforce, more opportunities will become available. Consider preparing yourself now. Are there any challenges or opportunities at your current workplace that you can tackle to demonstrate more of your abilities to your boss? Or, do you have a great idea that you'd like to have the team try to implement? Volunteer to lead a cross-function team or project to get practice and prove yourself.

❏ **Consider advancing in your role someplace else.** Sometimes personal ambitions are not aligned with available opportunities at your employer. If you've talked with your supervisor and the change you want is not available within a time frame that matches your expectations, you may have to make a change. If you can, check out other departments or companies that may have more room for advancement and the compensation you want.

Questions to Ask Yourself

Do you and your manager agree on your contributions and progress?

- What needs to change?

What are your top three priorities in your job or career now?

- Money?
- Job growth?
- Time?

1.

2.

3.

Do you feel you are where you need to be right now to reach your current career goals?

- Yes? No?
- Partially? Why did you select your answer?

If not, where do you think you need to be in terms of your career?

Exercise 2
Setting Priorities

List the top three things that will be important for you—
personally and/or professionally—in the next six to 12
months.

1.

2.

3.

Have at least two conversations with someone you trust
about how you accomplish these goals. Who will you ask?

1.

2.

Are you having trouble making a decision?

Sometimes a pros and cons list may not be enough—especially when you may place a higher value on certain aspects of your job or career. Try the following exercise that requires you to prioritize and weigh your options.

Directions:
1. List your choices in the choice columns.
2. List the key decision factors as a list in the left column.
3. If a key factor is very important, give it an importance multiplier. For example, if commute time is most important, you may want to give it a multiplier effect of 10. Give the best role a score of "1" and the least a score of "0." If they are the same, both get a "1" score.
4. Tally your score.
5. The highest score will help you decide your top priorities and serve as a starting point for your discussion or negotiation.
6. Once completed, discuss the results with someone you trust.

Decision: Example - Deciding to leave a job.

	Importance Multiplier (IM)	Choice One: Current Job		Choice Two: New Job	
	(Score: 1-10)	Score	Score with IM	Score	Score with IM
Short Commute	10	0	0	1	10
Pay Increase	5	0	0	1	5
Growth	5	0	0	1	5
Perks	0	1	0	1	0
Good Manager	10	1	10	0	0
Benefits	10	1	10	0	0
Company Culture	5	0	0	1	5
New Challenge	5	0	0	1	5
Stability	5	1	5	1	5
Travel	-10	0	0	1	-10
Scope of Role	2	1	2	1	2
New Skill Set	0	1	0	1	0
Mission	2	1	2	0	0
Total:		*5*	*28*	*11*	*27*

Decision: Example - Deciding to leave a job.

	Importance Multiplier (IM)	Choice One: Current Job		Choice Two: New Job	
	(Score: 1-10)	Score	Score with IM	Score	Score with IM
Total		5	28	11	27

In this example, if all things were equal, moving to the new job seems like an easy decision with a score of "11." However, when factors such as travel, benefits, and mission come into play, the decision to stay in your current role with a multiplier score of "28" may win out and lead you to engage in a bit more thought about what really matters at this point.

Are you having trouble making a decision?

Sometimes a pros and cons list may not be enough—especially when you may place a higher value on certain aspects of your job or career. Try the following exercise that requires you to prioritize and weigh your options.

Directions:
1. List your choices in the choice columns.
2. List the key factors as a list in the left column,
3. If a key factor is very important, give it an importance multiplier. For example, if commute time is most important, you may want to give it a multiplier effect of 10. Give the best role a score of "1" and the least a score of "0." If they are the same, both get a "1" score.
4. Tally your score.
5. The highest score will help you decide your top priorities and serve as a starting point for your discussion or negotiation.
6. Once completed, discuss the results with someone you trust.

Decision:			
	Importance Multiplier (IM)	Choice One: Current Job	Choice Two: New Job
	(Score: 1-10)	Score	Score with IM	Score	Score with IM
Total:					

Practical Suggestions for Supervisors of Millennials/Gen Y

Many of your Millennial workers are finding themselves in a great place, while others may be struggling or thinking of something else. Make a commitment to help your employees find satisfaction in terms of performance and connection with others.

- ❏ **Offer constructive feedback when it is warranted.** Generation Y is used to instant feedback for their ideas due to their frequent use of social media during their formative years. Give them what they need to fully perform what you're asking of them, including encouraging words. Be thoughtful about requests for better or different work, and make sure you also share truthful assurances regarding what you appreciate about their work.

- ❏ **Be clear about their options.** Be sure to let them know they are valued in their current role and be willing to be open and realistic about their career prospects. Whether you are presenting job options within your team or laterally within your organization, encourage your employees to explore and do what they can to position themselves for moving on if they have mastered their current position. Coach them to move sideways when you can, and be supportive of their choices to move on if they do.

❐ **Support family and work-life balance.** Allow flexibility with work schedules. Relationships and happiness are extremely important to your Millennial workers, so be careful to not treat these as afterthoughts in your interactions with your team members. Gen Y-ers who feel that you value what they value will be more satisfied and more likely to go the extra mile for you.

❐ **Create a platform for problem-solving.** Make time to listen to your Millennials and get their ideas about what's going on with the department and the company. Answer their hard questions as best you can and address their complaints and concerns. Keep an open mind as you solicit their input.

Questions for Supervisors of Millennials/Gen Y to Consider

Have you checked with your Millennial employee to understand their perspectives on their careers and their tenure with your company?

Do your Millennial employees have a realistic view of their career options? What can you do to gain alignment?

How accurately do you represent your organization to your Millennials?

Do you know the reasons your employees leave or stay? Are there differences by generation group? What can you do to change or influence the outcome?

4

WORK ENVIRONMENT PREFERENCES

> If I had a regular week, like 70 percent work, 30 percent leisure, I think, would be fair. I think what's most important for me and most difficult, I think, sometimes, is just consistency.
>
> **Gen Y Male**

> I really enjoy my work and it doesn't always feel like work. Sometimes it feels more like leisure.
>
> **Gen Y Female**

As companies seek ways to get the most out of their workforce and build leaders, there has been great attention paid to the largest generation in the workplace—Millennials. Recent articles have a lot to say about significant trends in the American workplace, several in particular that involve the Millennial generation in specific ways. Information access and technology is transforming the workplace, and Millennials are in the thick of it. Millennials are also the most educated generation to date, bringing skill and expertise to bear early in their career tenures. They are starting conversations about cultural diversity in the workplace. At the same time, Gen Y has a distinct perspective when it comes to compensation and pay.

Members of Gen Y in the workforce are somewhere between 21 and 36, just getting started or a couple jobs into their career. What type of workplace do they want to thrive in every day? What are they looking for? Let's take a look at the current American workplace and the Millennial preferences that are shaping it, in terms of their idea of an ideal job, and in terms of an ideal supervisor.

Recent Trends in the American Workplace

INFORMATION AND TECHNOLOGY

No one can deny that technology has created astonishing change in the work environment, including how, when, and where we work. Remote work arrangements have been facilitated by the instant exchange and accessibility of information in its many forms, from documents to audio/video to live feed interactions across the globe. According to the U.S. Bureau of Labor Statistics, in 2015, about 24% of workers did some or all of their work from home.[39] Flex-time, creative work spaces, and outsourcing are also changing daily work, and there are more resources available in terms of in-house services to enhance the health and productivity of employees.[40]

Millennials, coming of age as technology brought these changes to the process of work, strongly prefer user-friendly interfacing with the software and apps they use on a daily basis. Some reports show that they prefer to solve their own problems and move away from apps and sites where they can't easily resolve issues regarding function or purchase, finding their answers in the vast repository of other options available. This tendency has driven demand for high-quality user experience in tech development.[41]

Even if they have to find, produce, or tweak it themselves, Millennials expect to use specialized software such as industry-specific accounting or inventory or customer management systems, or training software, which can interface across critical systems in the workplace, far beyond the use of Microsoft Word and Excel. The proactive supervisor can take advantage of input regarding technology from their Millennial employees, who will be adept at coming up with both small process tweaks as well as custom innovations to drive company productivity.[42]

Pay

Considering that Millennials are 50% more likely to be college educated than earlier generations and they are the significant driving force behind a 70% boom in workplace productivity,[43] there is some logic that would lead to the perception that Gen Y will be the highest paid generation to date. However, many studies are finding that this is not the case.

Examining data from the U.S. Census Bureau's Current Population Survey, one researcher looked at the annual earnings for a Millennial in 2014, a Gen X member in 2004, and a Baby Boomer in 1984, each earner at the age of 30. With the numbers adjusted for inflation, today's 30-year-olds are bringing in as much as a 30-year-old in 1984, that is, $19.30 per hour. Ten years ago, 2004's 30-year-old earned a dollar more per hour than today's worker.[44] The Young Invincibles organization examined Federal Reserve data for 25- to 34-year-olds in 1989 (now younger Baby Boomers) and for 25- to 34-year-olds in 2013 (now Millennials), establishing that today's Millennials are making about 20% less than their parents did, and have a lower net worth, while being more educated.[45]

It is an undeniable reality that, for any number of reasons, those coming of age during the financial crisis of 2008 found themselves taking jobs at depressed wages, which has continued to hinder their ability to attain the same living standards as the earlier generational cohorts.

This said, other reports find that Millennials are willing to take less pay and other benefits (such as retirement, medical insurance, paid time off, and ownership of a part of the company) in exchange for better work/life balance, which includes career development, meaningful work, and a certain company culture. Six in 10 Gen Y members would give up $7,600 on average in exchange for more ideal "quality of work life."[46] Compensation is important, but there is more flexibility in housing, transportation, and consumption options than there is at work. Once a job offer is accepted, other potential options are eliminated, such as other possible companies to learn from and contribute to, a different group of co-workers, and a different desired workplace culture.

DIVERSITY

At the same time that technology is changing the day-to-day face of the workplace, there is also increased diversity in age and background of coworkers. Millennials are more comfortable conversing about diversity and inclusion at work than Gen X and the Boomers. In fact, 47% of Gen Y considers diversity and inclusion to be important factors when thinking about a new job, compared to 33% of Gen X and 37% of Baby Boomers. While employees of all ages agree that employers placing an emphasis on diversity and inclusion (D & I) makes their place of employment better, Millennials tend to say that such practices make the workplace a better place to work and increase opportunities for all employees. Gen X and Baby Boomers are more likely to say that the boss is implementing "D & I" policies in order to make the company look better to outsiders and because of outside pressure.[47]

According to the U.S. Census Bureau, 44% percent of Millennials identify as a minority race or ethnic group other than non-Hispanic, single-race white.[48] Eleven percent of Millennials are children of immigrant parents, accounting for the largest number of second-generation Americans than any previous generational cohort.[49]

EDUCATION

Americans believe that it takes both technical and social savvy to navigate the workplace successfully. Competence with computers and being able to work with people from widely diverse backgrounds rank as most important, ahead of training in writing, communication, math, and science.[50]

U.S. employment trends point to increasing demand for advanced education, training, and experience for a wider range of industries, and a decline in need for physical and manual skill. Education and healthcare are experiencing the greatest industry growth, helping to create this need for greater education and training. Fifty-four percent of workers, representing all education levels, agree that their future success at work will involve continuing skill development, predominantly in further formal education.[51]

In 2010, Pew Research reported that half of Millennials wanted to go to college. Thirty-two percent intended to go to graduate school or a professional college. Sixty-five percent of those who had quit wanted to go back. Of the 48% that did not continue in school, 36% said they could not afford it, and 35% said they didn't have time—likely because they were too busy working. Only 14% said they didn't need any more education. One in 10 Millennials were working full-time and going to school.[52]

Seven years later, Generation Y is indeed the best educated cohort to date in America: one third of Millennials age 26–33 have achieved a Bachelor's degree or higher.[53] Twenty-one percent of men and 27% of women age 18–33 had completed at least a Bachelor's degree.[54]

As the economy shifts to a knowledge base rather than a labor base, those who have not pursued schooling beyond high school are having a much harder time making ends meet. They face consistently lower wages and higher unemployment rates, much more so than did Generation X and Baby Boomers who had only high school education.[55]

In my study, 1% had less than a high school diploma, and 16% had ended their education with high school. By contrast, 28% had completed a Bachelor's degree and 24% had gone on to do post-graduate to post-doctorate work.

Education Attainment for Gen Y	
Completed some high school	1%
High school graduate	16%
Completed some college	17%
Associate degree	14%
Bachelor's degree	28%
Completed some postgraduate	5%
Master's degree	14%
Ph.D., law, or medical degree	4%
Other advanced degree	1%

Millennials and Work Preferences

I can't imagine ever wanting to retire. I like working. I can't imagine not working and feeling fulfilled.

Gen Y Female

Give me more chances to step into leadership roles at work.

Gen Y Female

Give us more development opportunities and more direction as to what training we should be doing to enhance our skills.

Gen Y Female

Where are Millennials working? Sixty-eight percent of the survey respondents were employed at for-profit businesses at survey time. Twelve percent were in academic settings and another 12% in non-profit. The 8% remaining were working in government roles.

Given the chance to select the option that most closely matched their job title, one quarter of the group reported *management* or *director* and 8% reported *vice president* or *senior vice president, C level executive,* or *president/CEO*. There was one *owner/entrepreneur* among the respondents, and one *intern*. Seven percent were *teachers* or *professors*. The other possible categories included *assistant, analyst, associate, representative, specialist, coordinator,* and *other.*

Corresponding with current employment trends, the most represented industry was healthcare and medical-related at 15%. The next most represented industry was education at all levels, for 13.5%. Twelve percent of respondents were employed in retail. Construction and manufacturing accounted for 11% of the respondents, followed by information services and data at 7%, finance and insurance at 5%. Eighteen percent of the respondents were in agriculture, forestry, fishing, or hunting; arts, entertainment, or recreation; broadcasting; communications and public relations; government and public administration; computer and electronics manufacturing; hospitality; legal and marketing.

What kind of hours are Millennials putting in? Two percent of respondents (all female) said they were not working (in between roles) at the time of the survey, and 3% said they preferred not working.

Fewer than 6% of the Gen Y respondents worked less than 20 hours per week, and 7% said that fewer than 20 hours a week would be ideal. The majority of Millennials, 57%, are working 21–40 hours a week, and 59% said that they would prefer a 21- to 40-hour work week. Thirty-five percent are working 41 or more hours per week, while only 31% want to be working this much.

Hours Preferred for Gen Y	
I prefer not to work	3%
Under 20 hours per week	7%
21-40 hours per week	59%
41-50 hours per week	27%
51-60 hours per week	3%
60+ hours per week	1%

More females than males reported working 21–40 hours per week, 58% to 55%, and the same percentages for both were working 41–50 hours—28%. Eight percent of males and 6% of females were working 51 or more hours per week.

Twelve percent of men indicated that they would find less than 20 hours ideal, alongside 3% of women. Fifty-four percent of men compared to 63% of women found 21–40 hours a week ideal, and 26% of men compared to 28% of women thought that 41–50 hours a week would be ideal. At the same time, more females than males, 4% to 3%, stated that they preferred not to work.

Aside from the sweet spot of 21–40 hours a week, Gen Y is working more than they want to work. This corresponds with the Millennial preference for work/life balance, while having to work enough hours to pay their dues in terms of career obligations and earning a living to pay their bills.

Hours Preferred for Gen Y, by Gender		
	Men	Women
I prefer not to work	3%	4%
Under 20 hours per week	12%	3%
21-40 hours per week	54%	63%
41-50 hours per week	26%	28%
51-60 hours per week	4%	1%
60+ hours per week	1%	1%

Gen Y and Ideal Job Tenure

Eighteen percent of the respondents of a February 2016 survey by Job-vite indicated that they change jobs every one to three years, and 16% percent will change jobs in four to five years. Millennials are reported to have the highest serial employee rate: 42% change jobs every one to three years for those 18 to 29 years of age. Fifty-five percent of Millennial women in particular will change jobs every one to three years.[56]

How do the Millennials in my study compare? Thirty percent of the Millennial respondents have been at their current position for three to five years, 34% of the men and 26% of the women. Twenty-seven percent overall have been with their current company one to two years, 24% of the men and 28% of the women. They plan to stick around more than the national average stated above; however, 10% intend to stay where they are for one to two years, and 23% intend to stay where they are for three to five years, for a total of 33%. This breaks down into 37% for men planning to stay with their current employers for one to five years and 29% of women planning to stay where they are for the same one- to five-year span.

Planned Tenure for Gen Y	
10+ Years	39%
6-10 Years	21%
3-5 Years	23%
1-2 Years	10%
Less Than 1 Year	7%

Planned Tenure for Gen, Y by Gender		
	Men	Women
10+ Years	39%	38%
6-10 Years	22%	20%
3-5 Years	26%	20%
1-2 Years	10%	9%
Less Than 1 Year	3%	13%

Twenty-five percent of the study participants had been with their current employer for six to 10 years, 27% of males and 24% of females. This represents roughly a quarter of Millennial employees who have stayed put five years longer than the national average of job tenure.

Gen Y Planning to Stay with Current Employer Six or More Years, by Gender	
Men	Women
61%	58%

What's the longest job tenure of Millennials in the survey? Seven percent of both males and females had already been with their current employer for 10 or more years. It is remarkable and encouraging to note that 39% and 38% respectively intend to be with their current employer for 10 or more years. These Millennials have found a place to flourish professionally and personally and are invested in a solid future where they are.

At the same time, 7% indicated intentions of leaving their current employer after less than a year's tenure: 3% of males and 14% of females. I requested a reason for leaving from those who said they would leave before a year was up. The responses ran as follows:

- *Not happy with current job*
- *I would like a new job at a different employer*
- *It's not a healthy environment*
- *I am currently conducting a search for new employment*
- *Because I am going to work in my career after graduating*
- *Need a change*
- *Plan to get degree*
- *Don't like my employer*
- *Another job opportunity with more room for advancement*
- *I dislike my job*

The most common reason given was dislike for the situation, which lines up with the Millennials' priority of a work/life balance, being able to like their work and their employment culture.

Gen Y and the Boss

Most jobs these days require high levels of leadership and communication skill in order to successfully coordinate teams and projects. Flexibility and willingness to try new things are critical. Supervisors are in key positions to teach their younger employees these crucial skills and draw on their more experienced workers to help create the most productive and amenable culture possible.[57]

As with any generation cohort, Millennials have very clear ideas about what constitutes a good boss and what is unacceptable. Some of the most important things supervisors can do are to be open and appreciate the kind of worker their Millennial employee is and spend time getting to know him or her as an individual with a unique personality and set of skills.

Gen Y values and finds great benefit in interaction without hierarchy and a free exchange of information that leads to negotiation and solutions. In the workplace, this translates into great capacity for feedback, both positive reinforcement and constructive criticism, and the preference to discuss issues without top-down criticism and orders. As would any diligent employee, Millennials want sufficient instruction in order to accomplish their tasks, and they want to be directed and challenged toward success as well. Millennials see supervisors less as authority figures who must be obeyed and treated with deference and more as lead team members who help make the workplace function well. Coworkers are collaborating equals to support and be supported by. Ultimately, happiness is found in meaningful work and emotional connection and satisfaction that things in life are going as well as possible.

In this book, I wanted to focus on what Millennials want in a boss and how certain management practices can influence the Gen Y journey at work.

How Gen Y Feels about Their Boss

Study participants had the opportunity to rate their current supervisor as a leader using *excellent*, *good*, *average*, *poor*, or *awful*. Compared to the other generational cohorts in the study, Gen Z was the only cohort with a greater percentage (84%) than Gen Y that indicated they thought that their boss was an *excellent* or *good* leader; fewer Gen X (70%) and Baby Boomers (66%) gave an *excellent* or *good* rating.

Seventy-six percent of Gen Y participants considered their boss an *excellent* or *good* leader; 37% of respondents rated their boss *excellent* as a leader, and 39% rated the boss as *good* as a leader. The remaining 24% selected *average*, *poor*, or *awful* to describe their boss.

Gen Y Rating of Their Boss as a Leader	
Excellent	36%
Good	41%
Average	16%
Poor	4%
Awful	3%

Along with their rating, participants were asked to explain their selections. There were many reasons given for an *excellent* boss rating. The answers given the most had to do with support and care for individuals (most frequently mentioned), excellent leadership skills (next most mentioned), knowledge of the business, and good communication. Other Gen Y respondents had the following to say:

- *Advocates for her staff, funny and easygoing*
- *Because she cares about each employee and his dignity*
- *She is extremely helpful, motivating and wants to see you succeed*
- *Very understanding and fair*
- *Helps you anytime*
- *Friendly*
- *They are honest and trustworthy and very knowledgeable*
- *She knows her job inside and out, is an excellent teacher, strives to make everyone better and can take control in chaotic situations*
- *She took the time to listen and understand me and help me grow.*
- *Have a transparent communications approach towards all employees, especially in sharing decisions about whether a person should have a promotion or not. Also, good quality in personality.*

Several participants had no problem identifying what they disliked the most about their bosses.

- *The power to simply not care*
- *He is a narcissist jerk*
- *Out of touch owner manager with a big attitude*
- *Hardly ever present. Loquacious and unproductive.*
- *Incompetent*
- *There is no support or concern for employees*

In my study, Gen Y respondents gave specific feedback as to what their supervisors could do that they felt would help them to succeed in their current role. Respondents were given the opportunity to answer these two questions: 1) **Please list one thing you would like your supervisor to START doing to help you be more successful in your role**; and 2) **Please list one thing you would like your supervisor to STOP doing to help you be more successful in your role.**

Only 6% said that there was nothing they could ask their supervisor to start doing that would increase their chances of job success, which suggests a general sense of comfort with the approach and style of their current manager.

What Does Gen Y Want Their Bosses to Start Doing?

Gen Y respondents in my study shared very specific feedback on how their managers can help them be more successful in their roles. The most common response had something to do with wanting their supervisors to actually lead, including pleas to be bolder in disciplinary action.

- *Try being more of a leader rather than just "going with the flow"*
- *Step up to the plate and not let other employees step over her*
- *Being there more often*
- *Be present at the facility so they may accurately provide helpful feedback.*
- *Taking charge and being more assertive and vocal leader*

- *Grow a backbone with co-workers who won't pull their own weight*
- *Be a leader and maybe work*
- *Disciplining coworkers*
- *Grow a backbone*

Fourteen percent specifically wanted their bosses to help them succeed where they were and advance by teaching them what they needed to know, pointing them in the right direction, and simply training them.

- *Training*
- *I would like him to help me with things I might not know much about.*
- *Offer training*
- *Teach me new techniques*
- *Teach me more about being a mod*
- *Give us more tips*
- *Better instruction*
- *I think that my supervisor should better train the people that are coming in as a new employee.*
- *Teach more*
- *Find projects for me to do to build my resume.*
- *Continue to give me advice and guide me in the right direction*
- *Help me find learning opportunities*
- *Give us more development opportunities and more direction as to what training we should be doing to enhance our skills*
- *Answer phone calls, so I could get an answer on what's best to do*
- *Giving me input on how to excel.*
- *Training me in other areas to see what my full potential is*
- *Help us by showing us better techniques to get our work done faster and more efficient.*
- *Provide me with better tools to exceed. Demonstrate concern for my growth in the position.*

Ten percent wanted more direct feedback as to strengths and weaknesses, correction, and constructive criticism. Some asked to simply be kept in the loop more. Some wanted their bosses to listen more.

These responses confirm for us that Millennials do indeed strongly desire bosses they can respect, leaders who will truly lead, and provide situations and feedback that will help them to succeed.

Six percent of the respondents indicated that they wanted more responsibilities and leadership opportunities. Six percent each wanted better pay or promotion. Another 6% wanted the manager to adjust hours assigned so that work could be done, workloads lessened, dependability demonstrated, and schedules be distributed fairly. Another 6% asked for better communication, clearer objectives, and better delegation.

Other repeated comments included requests to cease micromanaging and trust that things were getting done right, and that the boss respect other management styles. *Listen to me, be nicer,* and *care about employee*s was requested, as were organization, teamwork, and help from the boss. Four respondents requested acknowledgement and appreciation. Two wanted transparency and honesty from their bosses.

Two respondents mentioned that they wanted help with education issues, including more time to get a degree and help with tuition payments. Two wanted their superiors to help them with personal savings plans and investing in the company. Finally, reflective of the Millennial desire for specific work-culture situations, several offered a number of ways that things could be made better, including:

- *Make things more fun*
- *Make it fair for both guy and girl employees to talk together*
- *Assure equality between employees*
- *One thing I would like my supervisor to start doing is ask more questions as to how we can improve our work space*

The "office culture" matters to Millennials, and it includes things that other generations would consider personal issues for which the workplace isn't responsible. However, the supervisor who can do even a little bit toward understanding and facilitating these workplace preferences will have a much better chance of retaining employees who want to work hard and succeed where they are now.

What Does Gen Y Want Their Bosses to Stop Doing?

A surprising 24% of Millennials couldn't list anything they wanted their boss to stop doing in order for them to be more successful, although the rest had a wide array of responses. For the most part, they expressed desire for the same things in these answers that they did in the answers to the question about what the boss could start doing, just using different words. Along the lines of those who wanted their bosses to grow a spine and take care of business, four individuals wanted their supervisor to stop being such a coward and pushover. Similarly, 8% wanted their supervisor to stop being absent, stop being lazy, and stop being unengaged.

Six percent wanted their boss to stop micromanaging them, and another 6% wanted their boss to stop nagging and putting demands on them. Three individuals wanted their bosses to stop making assignments outside their roles.

There were many requests to stop disrespectful behavior such as glaring, speaking down, shutting down employee ideas, being critical, being judgmental, and being sarcastic. Favoritism, gossiping, yelling, rudeness, ignoring issues, negative attitude, and unprofessional or immature behavior were other things employees wanted stopped. Two needed their supervisors to stop trying to prevent their promotion; two wanted their managers to stop standing in the way of progress:

- *Discouraging me from pursuing a specific avenue because he thinks I'm inadequate and won't reach success.*
- *Not letting me go with higher office*
- *Doing things the old fashion way and embrace the new ways of using technology*
- *Preventing progress/change*

Other responses include:

- *Stop reassignment of my subordinates.*
- *Stop chatting so much with the employees about personal rather than professional agenda.*
- *Stop passing off ridiculous tasks that have no significant impact on our company.*
- *Maybe stop having to review everything.*
- *Stop ordering us around and become a leader*
- *One thing I would like my supervisor to stop doing is being too stubborn.*
- *Complaining to everyone that no one respects her*
- *He needs to stop tripping*
- *He is excessively chatty. So I would like less of that so I can be more productive.*
- *Stop blaming other people for things he was supposed to do and forgot to do.*
- *Patronizing*
- *Hinting at future changes without detail or any idea when things will change or even if they will change. It just creates uncertainty and employees worry about things that may never happen.*
- *Stop being dumb*
- *Being in the office for a long period of time, busy yes. But go out sometimes and make conversations.*
- *Making a big deal of small, exceedingly rare oversights*

As stated before, the workplace atmosphere is very important to Millennials, not just the work they're doing. A good boss can go a long way toward creating employee satisfaction simply by being a positive, engaged, and proactive leader.

A high percentage of satisfaction with the boss and high expressed intent to stay with current employers suggests strongly that many Millennials have found their place to stay, contribute, and develop. This should be encouraging to supervisors who perhaps dread hiring Millennials with the thought that they are impossible to please and will be quitting as soon as they're on-boarded. Understanding what your Gen Y workers really want and accommodating them as much as possible will make them happy and productive members of your team.

Implications for Work Success and Career Paths

The historical economic data of the 2000s recession explains Millennial difficulty with finding good jobs, coping with school, and making-ends-meet debt, and putting off marriage, family, and home buying. Thus, the money and advancement are important. Adeptness with technology and the efficiency that it offers makes them question the need to arrange work the way it's always been, whether in cubicles or at certain hours. It is clear that Millennials have a definite set of priorities that define some of the parameters of their careers.

Gen Y is ready to commit for the long haul. They want to make the world a better place, at least their part of it. They want to work with a mentor or coach rather than a superior. Or they'd prefer to work for themselves. They prefer collaboration to competition. They want freedom to work when and how it makes sense to them, instead of the tradition well-established workplace practices.[58]

My study shows that if the work, the compensation, their boss, or the social atmosphere at work are not good, Millennials have no problem moving on to a better situation.

■ ■ ■

Consider the following statements:
"The interview was pretty good the other day, but when I asked about performance reviews and promotion schedules, they just glanced at each other, gave some lame nonsensical answer and moved on to the next question. So there's another place I can plan on just swimming along without guidance until I get so frustrated I quit. How can you run a business without your people knowing what it takes to succeed?" – Gen Y Female

"I can hardly keep my cool sometimes. Why are these kids always chatting over the cubicle walls about things that have nothing to do with work? Some soccer meetup they have going on, her kid, his dad's cancer… If they need to be friends, they need to do it after work. I have a department to run here." – Baby Boomer Male

"So I told our HR manager how I saw on Facebook how the recent hurricane left one of our coworkers homeless and suggested that we may want to perhaps crowdsource to raise money to help them out. He just stared at me for a bit, then said something about not being really sure that was appropriate. So much for our company values of caring about people. It matters, doesn't it?" – Gen Y Male

"I'm losing my workers left and right and I don't know why. They come, work hard, stay for three or so years, then they're gone. I've bent over backward to get them better benefits, done some remodeling around the place, let them set their schedules, but nothing seems to make them happy to stay. Just when they finally know what's going on, I lose them." – Gen X Female

The statements above demonstrate that we all enter the workforce with our life experiences and unique points of view. However, it's equally clear that solutions to frustrations in the workplace must involve sitting down to ask pointed questions about not just priorities, but how those priorities can be implemented. What is important and why is it important? And both sides need to participate equally with the intention of true discovery and commitment to letting change happen.

■ ■ ■

Practical Suggestions for Millennial/Gen Y Employees

Not everyone has a parent, manager, supporter, or mentor to help guide and shape their career. Most of us are left to figure it out along the way. As you know, no workplace will ever be perfect. However, a workplace can function effectively as long as expectations are aligned. And, when everyone has a chance to express opinions and be heard, and work toward solutions and compromise. My study shows that most people have high expectations of their managers and of the company or organization where they work. It's just that the picture of success can be different from person to person.

- ❏ **Sometimes you have to compromise.** You may also have to just accept conditions as they are and develop a plan to succeed with the tools available to you. Compromise does not have to mean losing; perhaps you can find middle ground. Also, change may take time. If you see forward progress, don't give up.

- ❏ **Be accountable.** Be sure you're doing what you're asked to do completely and as well as you can. Requests for change won't be received if you're not doing your part in the eyes of your boss. If you need instruction, you may have to ask in plain language. If you can, volunteer for extra challenges to demonstrate your commitment to the company and your own success.

- ❏ **Learn to navigate office politics.** Office politics. You can't escape it or ignore it. But you can build skills to better manage it. By now, you may have experienced or heard about occasions where the less talented, but most favored person prevails or a seemingly unfair situation occurs. Understand and be thoughtful about building your own informal and formal networks. This is not about popularity, but you will need to have access to people with information or influence who can help you. Invest in ways to expand your emotional quotient or "EQ" (also referred to as emotional intelligence) so that you are equipped with tools to read and navigate the unwritten social cues that exist in every organization, and can manage your response and reputation accordingly.

❐ **Be careful and clear about what you ask for.** Managers are problem-solvers. If you bring a problem with the solution you are seeking, you may get what you want. But if you are not clear, the solution may not be what you expect. Also, if you don't do your homework and present something that is totally outside of what the organization has done before, your request could end up dead on arrival.

Questions to Ask Yourself

What do you love about your employer and your role?

Are you celebrating your successes? If not, why?

Do you have relationships throughout the organization (e.g., from the reception, inside and outside of your department, different levels within the organization)?

Are you managing your stress in a positive way?

- Are you managing your work and life priorities well?
- What can you say no to?
- Are you managing your health?
- Are you making time for your friends, personal interests, and family?

Exercise 3
Finding Success on the Job

Part 1: Be clear about what you want in your career right now. List the top three considerations you had in mind when you accepted the job offer with your current employer. Note whether those ideas are still important or if your thoughts have changed.

1.

2.

3.

Part 2: Put your thoughts into action. Now ask yourself what you can do to help create any change you want, and if you can stay if things don't change. Have a conversation about your thoughts with someone your trust.

1.

2.

3.

Part 3. Be intentional about managing your reputation.

1. What do you think that you are good at doing?

2. Ask at least five people what are you known for being good at doing.

3. What is your passion?

4. What are your values?

5. Invest in objective measures of your competencies. Take an assessment to understand your strengths and areas for development. Examples include: DISC, Myers-Briggs, and Strength Finders.

6. What is your level of engagement at work beyond your job?
- Do you participate in social or after-work activities?
- Do you volunteer for or are you asked to do special projects?
- Do you deliver on your commitments?

7. What is your level of engagement in your chosen profession? Do you stay current in developments in your field? Do you belong to and/or are you active in professional organizations that relate to your industry?

8. Are you careful and thoughtful about your social and online presence? Have you performed an online search of your name? Are you comfortable with what you found?

9. Summarize questions 1-8 into one paragraph. Refine the paragraph until you are comfortable that it reflects who you are and who you want to be known as by others. Summarize the paragraph into one sentence. Ask someone you trust if the statement you wrote rings true. Use this as your guidepost.

10. Review this list at least once a year.
- Find an accountability partner to keep you focused.
- Refine and revise as needed.

Practical Suggestions for Supervisors of Gen Y/Millennials

Although the issues that arise may seem trivial to you, your Millennial worker is wired to perform his or her best work when certain conditions are met. Facilitating an accommodating workplace can be your best productivity booster and retention tool.

- ❑ **Create an ideal work setting.** The work environment matters to Millennials. Whether it is the tone you set or the culture at your office, this generation isn't comfortable with a cold or sterile setting with a "punch the clock" and "heads down" style. They tend to see work as an extension of their lives. Flexibility in approach, location, hours, and atmosphere all make a difference in productivity, tenure, and loyalty.

- ❑ **Be generous with constructive feedback.** Remind yourself that your Gen Y worker is used to all sorts of input with which to evaluate and make decisions, and the most user-friendly resources will win out. Make professional feedback, company information, and appropriate training readily available. Plan ways to gather their ideas and utilize their preferences to make the workplace and work process as attractive and satisfactory as possible.

- ❑ **Provide training.** For many Millennials, the path to an ideal role was a journey. Now that they've arrived, they want to do well. Training is an investment in your employees and sets them up for success. The training can be done by you, via courses that your company provides or external sources. Don't wait for them to ask for training; consider making the investment in job skills and professional development to set them up for success.

- ❑ **Capitalize on their strengths.** Are you using each employee to their fullest? Try to arrange tasks and systems to utilize your Gen Y worker's skills to their fullest, adding challenges as well.

Solicit their ideas as to how to improve processes and make them responsible for implementing the change.

☐ **Be mindful that all your actions matter.** Command and control styles don't appear to play well with Gen Y. Employees pay close attention to how you conduct yourself. Your behavior and leadership will shape the future of your company and the workplace. A respectful and supportive supervisor will bring out your Gen Y workers' best efforts, and they can become your best long-term assets.

Questions for Supervisors of Millennials/Gen Y to Consider

What ways do you let your Millennial employees know what success and opportunities for advancement look like in your company?

What is your management style? Does it help or hinder the type of performance you are seeking?

How often do your coach your employees?

Are your actions and behaviors consistent?

Do you have crucial conversations with transparent feedback? Or, do you avoid the difficult conversations? If so, why?

How often you do celebrate wins?

What do you to manage your stress?

5

ATTITUDES ABOUT OTHER GENERATIONS AT WORK

They seem to have been born just 'knowing' everything there is to know about technology.

Baby Boomer Female

Searching for better jobs.

Gen X Female

Not afraid to do things outside the box and take risks.

Y Female

Gen Y seems to have the best of X and Baby Boomers. They take their job seriously but aren't usually as harsh.

Gen Z Female

Recently, there has been more attention placed on generation-related differences. When these differences are comprehended, bias can be identified and eliminated, and it is much easier to see what is required for the success of the project, the individual, the team, and the company. Human resources professionals and leaders who really want to bring out the best in all their workers invest time in looking at the different qualities that each employee brings to their workforce. They make an effort to understand the range of wants, needs, and goals that must be integrated into their organization to see success for the bottom line and for individuals. Overlooked disparities or opportunities can lead to conflict, while awareness of differences is the first step toward productive collaboration. Employers and employees both can make conscious efforts to understand each other's perspectives.

Of course, anyone can have difficulty seeing the negative characteristics, or stereotypes, associated with their own generation. One could easily imagine that it's harder for one generation to view another with more positive regard than negative. Even so, my research found a number of surprisingly generous intergenerational assessments.

They Said... We Said...

I invited the study participants to share their opinions about their coworkers in each generational group and asked *Considering the multigenerational workplace, what is the BEST thing about each generational group?* In other words, I gave each generation the chance to say something nice about every other generation to gain insights on the positive attributes of each generation group.

When the responses came in, it was evident how difficult it is to let go of certain negative biases. The responses, instead of strictly identifying positive things, were a mix of positive, negative, and neutral observations.

How Baby Boomers, Gen X, and Gen Z See Gen Y

In offering their opinions about Gen Y, the Baby Boomers, Gen X, and the Gen Z-ers stated all the common negative opinions about Millennials. However, there were many astute observations made by members of each generation identifying the positive and unique strengths Gen Y brings to the table.

The majority of comments centered on the Millennials' technical savvy and focus, noting a positive. *Their ability and willingness to embrace and adopt technology*—and a negative: *caught up in technology.* An assortment of expressions by each generation captured Millennial creativity and propensity for new ideas.

Many respondents also noted that Millennials are interested in education, wanting to learn everything they can, and that they are highly educated. A couple also said that they've noticed a focus on advancement and planning for retirement as positive identifying traits for Gen Y. The three generations also noted that Millennials tend to be more socially oriented, and that they are hardworking. On a lighter note, at least one respondent in each generation, including Gen Y, claimed that this generation had the best music.

Baby Boomer Perspective on Gen Y: While the tech-savviness, balance, and impact were noted, the Baby Boomers listed more of the negative traits: lazy, think everything should be handed to them, jump from company to company, want what they want, don't care about working, disrespectful and unappreciative, spoiled liberal brats.

Baby Boomer Insights
- *Technology background*
- *Wanting to make things better and easier*
- *Blending young ideas with maturity*
- *Are ok employees, tend to be job jumpers*
- *Not afraid to ask questions or to demand authenticity*
- *Teaches everyone else how the new tech can help us all*
- *Balance*

Gen X Perspective on Gen Y: Gen X identified more emotional personality traits, such as high-strung, sad, frank, shy, straightforward, courage, free-spirited, driven, and humble. Gen X also had a few choice words: lazy oversensitive crybaby techno zombies, acting like they know it all. A number of Gen X respondents also said specifically that they relate to Gen Y in age.

Gen X Insights
- *Take care of the environment*
- *New in workplace and potential to go far*
- *Innovative and optimistic*
- *Empathetic to those with kids*

Gen Z Perspective on Gen Y: Gen Z noted contradictions with their more senior Gen Y counterparts. Gen Z had very little negative to say about Gen Y. Gen Z identified with Gen Y in terms of fresh ideas and enthusiasm for new things. Some Gen Z perceived that Millennials grew up with both technology and minimal technology, had older and newer opinions, have both new and old traditions, modern/old school style. It seems that to Gen Z, Millennials are seen as elders.

Gen Z Insights

- *Change makers*
- *Give good advice but are also relatable*
- *This newer generation can still teach Gen Z*
- *They began & continue a great deal of the social justice campaigns we know today.*

INSIGHTS ABOUT HOW EACH GENERATION THINKS ABOUT THE OTHERS

	About Gen Z	About Gen Y	About Gen X	About Baby Boomers
Gen Z Female	They are innovative and don't mind challenging the status quo.	They have seen and survived a lot of worldwide change.	They are steady, reliable workers & people.	They began and continue a great deal of the social justice campaigns we know today.
Gen Y Female	Always looking for ways to incorporate the technology into projects and tasks.	Can always learn from them.	They can show you how to be humble and correct someone properly when they are wrong.	Not afraid to do things outside the box and take risks.
Gen X Male	Still young and impressionable to teach them good work ethics.	The best work ethics, friendly, down to earth.	Very responsible yet loose and easy-going.	Are fun, but can be down to business as well.
Baby Boomer Female	Less stressed and more laid back.	Content to do a good job and not necessarily looking to move up, therefore constant.	Experienced and usually good about sharing that experience.	Dependable and ambitious (still trying to move up)

How Gen Y Sees Themselves

Reflecting upon how members of Gen Y view the positive characteristics associated with themselves, the Millennial respondents had an array of answers that mirrored what the other three generations had to say about Gen Y. They consider themselves to be:

- *Creative*
- *Technologically savvy*
- *Culturally oriented*
- *Fighting for a better future*
- *Shaping the world*
- *Highly value education*
- *Eager*
- *Hardworking*
- *Socially oriented*

A few other comments offered additional attributes and insights into the Millennial mindset regarding their careers and contributions to the workplace:

- *Multidimensional*
- *Striving to become leaders*
- *Changing perceptions of work*
- *Not afraid to do things outside the box and take risks*
- *Cusp of making enough*
- *Right in their prime*
- *More cultural businesses*

Most of the comments were forward looking and positive. However, there was one stark reminder that many in this generation are having trouble finding jobs and wages commensurate with their education. They communicated it thus: *having a hard life*.

Taken together, the comments tell us that Gen Y considers themselves to be goal-oriented, open to diversity, confident, and ambitious explorers who are intent on changing what doesn't work in the world while securing their own futures.

How Gen Y Sees the Other Generation Groups

I also examined how Gen Y views their more senior and younger coworkers. For the most part, Gen Y described each generation in complimentary terms.

Millennial perspective on Baby Boomers: With very little negative to say, the Millennials summed up the soon-to-be-retired Baby Boomers with many repetitions of the following expressions:

- *Hard working*
- *Wise*
- *Better values*
- *Seasoned*
- *Ethics*
- *Life experiences*
- *Dedicated*
- *Retiring soon*
- *Responsible*
- *Traditional*
- *Enjoyed life more*
- *Money-wise*
- *Expanded the economy*

Perhaps the most complimentary homage offered to the Boomers was from a Gen Y Female: *Can always learn things from them that will always work until the end of time in the workplace and in real life.*

Millennial perspective on Gen X: For the most part, Gen Y spoke of their immediate elders, Gen X, with the same kind of respect that they used describing the Baby Boomers, providing variations of the following themes:

- *They are go-getters*
- *Hard workers*
- *Have great experience*
- *Knowledgeable*
- *Good work ethic*
- *Nice and friendly*
- *Excellent leaders*
- *Good humor*
- *Role models*
- *Willing to help*
- *Been there a while*

Interestingly, Millennials found Gen X to be more "mature" (i.e., old) than they found the Boomers.

- *Stuck in old ways*
- *Oldie music*
- *They're too conservative*
- *Do things old fashioned*

Although some found Gen X to be *contemporary* and *free thinkers*. At the same time, Millennials noted some Gen X responsibility for the beginning of change in workplace functioning and attitudes, such as those about work/life balance, and diversity.

- *Beginning of technology*
- *The way things changed from long ago*
- *Understand there's more to life than work*
- *They offer different ethnic groups and come up with more religious traditions.*

Millennial perspective on Gen Z: Gen Y noted Gen Z's youth, sometimes with understanding, sometimes with disparaging words, calling them out for laziness, immaturity, and cluelessness. However, more appreciated the Gen Z eagerness to learn and work and their adaptable, teachable spirit with lots of potential.

Most comments acknowledged considerable technical ability, some even acknowledging that Gen Z's competence outstripped their own.

- *Always a step ahead of the technology industry and always looking for ways to incorporate the technology in projects and tasks.*
- *This generation is very smart and are more talented than ever before.*
- *Think outside the box, more up to date on technology*
- *New Century with new Technology and greater accomplishments*

One Gen Y participant entered the following in each of the three spaces provided for comments about what they saw as most positive about each generation: *I don't like groups*. This clearly reflects the Millennial aversion to labels, logos, or other such distinctions.

In these verbatim replies, Gen Y shows themselves to be fairly level-headed and objective as well as observant. They don't begrudge acknowledging someone having better skills or different perspectives and give credit for hard work and experience.

Implications for Work Success and Career Paths

The workplace is changing and being driven by many factors, including shifts in generational values. I research the commonalities associated with the historical factors that help shape the values and preferences of the different generations to facilitate understanding, performance, cooperation and career success within the workplace. Workplaces that are staffed by all the generations can find a variety of perspectives. An appreciation of varying points of view will enable coworkers to anticipate and evaluate different scenarios and prepare for the future while staying grounded and realistic.

■ ■ ■

Consider the following statements:

"The senior leader in one group scares me. I can't just go up to her and ask her what she thinks about some of my ideas. She is too serious all the time and the unspoken rule is that you only communicate with your boss and those at your level." – Gen Y Male

"I was thinking of how we could get some of us to work remote hours without shorting staff on the phones if customers need us. I'd bring it up, but I bet you tomorrow's paycheck that half of us will love it and half of us will hate it, and you know who's going to be on which side." – Gen Y Female

"Why won't my younger employees open up about the ideas I know they have that would make things more efficient around here? I run a tight ship and efficiency is the name of the game, but none of them ever approach me or even write anything in the space on their performance reviews where I offer to let them share." – Gen X Female

"Our new manager just stormed out the door because she didn't get her way. In truth, she had a good idea, but the delivery was poorly executed. We all hate office politics. But learning how to navigate it is important. You have to build a network, know how to compromise and stop taking everything so personally. It's not always about you; we just don't have the budget right now. Millennials!" – Baby Boomer Male

■ ■ ■

In our age-diverse workforce, traditional ways of getting work done can be interpreted as "old-fashioned," as "classic," or "wise" and new ideas can be cast as "innovative," "native," or "value-added" depending on your point of view. Intentional exploration of the perspectives of other generations should be encouraged rather than dismissed without thoughtful consideration.

Questions to Ask Yourself

What can I learn from my coworkers and managers?

- Navigating the organizational and/or political culture?
- How to get things done?
- Technical skills or improvements?

What unique skills can I bring to the team or my organization?

What behaviors are you modeling? Are they positive?

Exercise 4
Building a Support Network

Think of two people within your organization who you admire and could help you discover and plan your career trajectory. One of those people could be your boss; another could be another employee who's been with the company for a long time.

Arrange to have a conversation with them during a time that does not interfere with your (or their) work responsibilities. Tell them you'd like to share what you admire about them and what they do, and ask them if they would be open to helping you to learn more.

Remember to follow up and to thank them for their help. If they decline your request, still be polite and find someone else to ask.

Who will you ask, and when will you ask?

What will you share about your goals and plans?

What next steps will you take?

Practical Suggestions for Supervisors of Gen Y/Millennials

While many or most processes are well established, innovation still plays a major role in gaining a competitive advantage. Make an effort to be open to contributions from Gen Y workers that stem from their day-to-day contributions, and their ability to approach things in new ways. Millennials are settling into their careers, but are still open to learning.

- ❏ **Share constructive feedback.** Lead Gen Y in continuing to develop a strong life-long work ethic by setting clear expectations and offering incentives and examples. Specific feedback and judicious correction are helpful, after you take the time to listen and understand where your younger workers are coming from.

- ❏ **Respect rules the day.** Gen Y is responsive to respectful, as-equals interaction, not inflexible command-and-control methods. They want to contribute meaningfully and be recognized for the value they add, but if they are demeaned or unheard, they will be less willing to respond well to what you're saying.

- ❏ **Accept that the workplace is an extension of their lives.** It is more than just a job. Expect to have to address things other than the work process. More and more employees find workplace culture to be as important, if not more important, than the work they do and the compensation they receive. Even if this seems irrelevant to you, remember that your Gen Y employees will look elsewhere if too much is unattractive about their whole work experience.

Questions for Supervisors of Millennials/Gen Y to Consider

How often do you provide constructive feedback about your employee's career trajectories at your company and in the industry generally?

How did you learn to navigate the workplace? Do you share that knowledge?

How do you create an environment where your employees can voice their own opinions? Is it resulting in productive conversation and improvements in culture and process?

6

CAREER ADVICE/REFLECTION

> If I really could go back in time I would tell myself to be more confident in my work and to always be prepared for anything in the workplace.
>
> **Gen Y Male**

> To take advantage of opportunities for growth and be open-minded.
>
> **Gen Y Male**

> Be confident in yourself and abilities. If you want something, go for it. The worst outcome leaves you where you are now.
>
> **Gen Y Female**

Born from 1981 to 1995, Millennials are now about 21 to 36 years old, just coming out of college to about 10 years into their working career. All of them have probably been around the block enough to have heard a great deal of career advice and put some of it into practice. With dreams and goals within reach, they are growing in their career, figuring out their best practices, skills, and preferences and learning important career and life lessons. They know what kind of wisdom resonates with them and the kind of leadership they respect and want to emulate.

It has been said that experience is the best teacher. If we heed the lessons that can be taught from success and failure, we can prepare for future success. To build on the collective experiences of the Millennials in this study, I asked the members of Gen Y *What is the best career advice that you have received?*

Learning from Others: Best Advice Gen Y Has Received

> Don't go to work to make friends. Go to work to contribute to your field. Don't focus on others. Be selfish. Focus on yourself.
>
> **Gen Y Female**

> The best career advice I have ever received is that it is okay to change careers multiple times. It's better to find the best career for you than to be stuck in a career that you can't achieve your maximum potential in.
>
> **Gen Y Female**

The most repeated sentiment was to never give up, which was considered the best advice by 12% of the respondents. The next most repeated nugget of advice was to find and do what you love, with 10% of the Millennial participants finding this most valuable. Eight percent of the respondents found the best advice in admonitions to put in the maximum effort to get the highest outcome, including *always give 100 percent and if you fall, get right back up, and to always treat your job as if it was your own business and never hold back.*

About 15% of the Millennials appreciated advice centered on managing personal boundaries and personal expectations. There were strongly worded encouragements to:

- Focus on yourself, your own business, and not others, *i.e., ignore chatter/advice from people who don't understand my path.*
- Expect mistakes, learn from them and move on, *i.e., always accept constructive criticism and remember you will never be perfect and will always need to improve an aspect of yourself.*
- Be flexible and willing to change your career or plan, *i.e., be adaptable and willing to change or grab new opportunities.*
- Ignore the naysayers, *i.e., don't allow people's ignorant perceptions of you to stop you from making it to the top.*

A few of the other jewels of wisdom offered include:

- *Become a powerful thinker*
- *Put yourself in the other guy's shoes*

- *Live like I am dying!*
- *To work harder until your idols become your rivals*
- *Own it*
- *Work in silence, let your noise be your success*
- *Make connections and don't be afraid to ask your connections questions*
- *This is just your first step*
- *If you are five min. early you are late. My mentor always said if you wait around for everyone else to step up before you step up you will always lose your spot*
- *To do the very best I can, and release myself from trying to control every little detail*

Lessons Gen Y Has Learned, So Far...

Self-reflection can be an important aspect of career development. It allows the opportunity to understand what is important and what are the barriers or distractions, and where one needs to go next. It exposes the key factors needed to plan a path forward. To get a perspective on which types of advice members of Gen Y found helpful, I asked them to offer advice for their younger selves. I asked *If you could go back in time, what advice would you give yourself at the beginning of your career?*

It is clear that Millennials are mindful of the impact of education, money, and career decisions on their lives. The category of best advice that was most often mentioned had to do with college, with 24 instances (15%). The responses were both general and specific:

- *Go to school for the right thing*
- *Stay in college*
- *Go back to school NOW!*
- *Improve your study habit*
- *Start earlier in getting college out of the way*

Four individuals named specific degrees that they would have told themselves to pursue from the start. This is a caution to be more mindful of the requirements for your career early on.

The next most common reply (8%) was a plea to start college earlier or get into their career earlier, and try to advance sooner. Eleven (7%) respondents mentioned money in their replies, eight of which were about saving more and earlier. Three gave themselves job hunting tips, and two called on themselves to think more clearly about what they really wanted and to make a better career decision.

- *Start sooner*
- *Get into this career earlier, and experience more job options early on*
- *Start seeking a higher position quicker*
- *Give myself a solid plan for saving money*
- *To think more about my strengths and what I really wanted to achieve before embarking on a career path*

Between three and eight percent of study participants would have told themselves to
- Work hard (8%)
- Be open minded and not to settle for less because of doubts that there is anything else or because of fear (7%)
- Learn more on the job (5%)
- Don't give up (5%)
- Be more verbally assertive (5%)
- Do something you like (4%)
- Be yourself (3%)

Five percent would have given themselves advice about getting along with others. Only four participants, 3%, had words about finding work/life balance.

"I hopped around jobs right out of college. Part of that was challenges faced finding any job, but I'd push myself to apply for more. I probably applied for 20 or so jobs out of college and thought that was tough. After hating my first two jobs, I applied for over 70 jobs in a month to find an opening at my current company, which aligns with my career goals. I had this sense of entitlement that I'd just get a great job when I graduated...and it's not that easy." – Gen Y Female

This last listed response embodies much of what Millennials faced in their first few jobs and face now in getting traction in their careers. However, the most common replies listed above make it clear that Millennials are mindful of what it takes. Admonitions to work hard, be open-minded, and not settle also remind us that this generation is well equipped to cope with their situation and attain what they want.

Implications for Work Success and Career Paths

Gen Y's eyes are wide open in terms of understanding how hard some of their cohort have struggled with poor job markets, college debt, and the overall and lasting effects of bear markets, yet they are still determined to chase their dreams and find success on their own terms. They know their success is up to their own hard work, and at the same time, they are committed to involvement with organizations they can respect and get behind.

Look again at the numbers of those above who most valued such admonitions to work hard, be open minded, learn more, not give up, etc. This is 34% of Millennials who find reminders of some kind of personal determination to be most helpful in looking forward. Probably the easiest thing supervisors and managers of Millennials can do is to genuinely and regularly encourage them to keep striving and not settle, to believe in themselves, and to go for what they want. Everyone needs encouragement, even those who are doing well.

Part of this encouragement is success adding to success. Both employees and their bosses can work together to find opportunities that enable Gen Y to accumulate accomplishments and additions to their skill sets. These achievements add not only to individual resumes, but also to overall company advancement.

Education figures strongly in the Gen Y psyche. It is understood as vitally important, even while the efforts for some have not resulted in higher pay or even work in the desired field. Both Millennials and their supervisors can find ways to support advancing education. First, there may be ways to recognize formal education attained in other fields by seeking ways to integrate that with current work. Secondly, for those who regret deeply that they are not working in the field they studied for, it is not too late to seek a change. And for those who do not have the formal education or who want to learn more, supervisors can make efforts to provide cross-training opportunities or provide company support (reimbursement of tuition or fees, and flex-time) for outside classes that supplement and strengthen current skills.

Questions to Ask Yourself

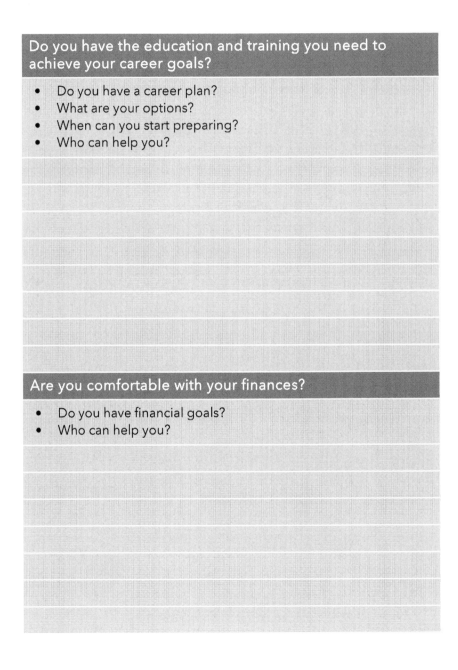

Do you have the education and training you need to achieve your career goals?

- Do you have a career plan?
- What are your options?
- When can you start preparing?
- Who can help you?

Are you comfortable with your finances?

- Do you have financial goals?
- Who can help you?

Exercise 5
Creating a Career Reassessment Map

As you build your career, it's often helpful to step back and assess whether you're where you thought you'd be. Complete the chart below and then ask for input from someone you trust.

1. Define the role and skills where you are now. List the skills used for your current role.

Current Role: Retail Associate

Skills Needed: working with customers, communication skills, time management, cashier experience, team player, flexibility

Current Role:

Skills Needed:

2. Identify the next roles you're interested in pursuing and list the skills you'll need for them. Examples can be found by searching employment websites or by talking to someone already in that role.

Next Role: Manager

Skills Needed: hire and develop staff, budget management, maintain employee work schedules, prepare reports, agility, interpersonal skills

Next Role:

Skills Needed:

3. Identify the training and/or education needed for your next role. Examples can be found by searching job descriptions or by talking to someone already in that role.

Next Role: Manager

Training/Education Needed: Bachelor's degree or equivalent

Next Role:

Training/Education Needed:

4. Identify the gaps in your background and training with the role you are seeking. Review the job description against your own experience and training to identify abilities you already have that you can transfer, or the skills you need to acquire. Note: it does not have to match 100%. List the areas where you need to gain more experience.

5. Create a plan to fill the gap. Think about ways that you can learn more about what the job entails and how you can get the experience and training you need. Talk with someone already in the role, or someone who supervises that role.

Example: Information interview with a manager at your organization, join a professional group, serve as a team leader or project leader to gain experience leading others, or speak with someone to help you brainstorm ideas about how to build out your next steps.

Who will you contact?

6. Make a plan with appropriate dates and milestones for attaining the skills for your next role, and find someone to keep you accountable and encourage you.

Practical Suggestions for Millennial/Gen Y Employees

Above all, remember that your Gen Y workers are still new in their careers. You can serve as a powerful role model, mentor, coach, and sponsor.

☐ **Be available to your Gen Y employees.** Let your employees know that you are interested in them and encourage them to ask questions. Make sure you have time set aside to be available to your team and inform them of your availability. When you meet with them, be prepared to receive their criticisms and suggestions as much as you'd like them to receive yours, and be prepared to be transparent about company policies and focus.

☐ **Build Gen Y's self-efficacy.** Self-efficacy relates to a person's belief in their ability to perform well and play a major role in how one approaches their job and problem-solves. Find out what's important to your Gen Y employee and acknowledge their contributions. Find ways to act as a sounding board while they try to evaluate and make decisions. Offer opportunities to even the most tentative person to try new things and take risks without fear of failure. Repeated experiences with success will build their confidence and performance over time.

☐ **Challenge them.** Point out areas in which this or that action can position them for advancement up or laterally, and encourage them to stretch themselves. Support ways your employee can increase their knowledge via training, course work, or stretch assignments.

7

EVERYONE HAS SOMETHING TO OFFER

> Set goals for yourself and what you want to see in the future. Work harder and longer in order to earn the money you need to be financially stable. Strive to become better every day and work your way up the chain of management.
>
> **Gen Y Female**

As we examine the multigenerational workplace, it's important to understand what can promote intergenerativity at work (i.e., sharing change across boundaries that normally separate discourse, and tapping the energy that can result from connecting otherwise divergent fields of human endeavor).[59] The key is for both Gen Y workers and their supervisors and coworkers to remember that there is always more than one perspective to be considered, each as legitimate as the next. A productive and positive growth experience needn't be considered an impossibility.

Everyone involved can acknowledge their own perspectives, but also deliberately set them aside in the interest of understanding others. Clear communication about desires and expectations can contribute to the establishment of common goals and the means of reaching them. The intent to understand and cooperate is essential, and refusal to step outside one's comfort zone or to compromise will nullify progress. This is true in the realm of personal development or that of team or organizational success.

Members of Gen Y are passionate about being involved and making a difference in ways that are important to them. Many want to commit to a single employer for a number of years, so it would be well worth the investment of training and mentoring Millennial employees. While some Millennials are still young and inexperienced in some ways, they have their areas of expertise to bring to the workplace. Others have been around long enough to have a solid grasp of their particular workplace culture and skill sets, and are ready to take on leadership roles. Their comfort with and knowledge of technology as well as familiarity with the "old school" can make workplace growth smoother than for those working from only one perspective.

Key Takeaways

Happiness, relationships, doing well in their role, compensation, and job satisfaction are most important for Gen Y, and because of this, a solid work/life balance will figure heavily into personal and career decisions. Inclusion and justice are also two lenses through which Gen Y evaluate job choices. Millennials consider themselves part of a bigger system within which they must find a way to live and contribute meaningfully. In this way, satisfying only themselves is not a given.

Gen Y believes that the American Dream is highly accessible to them, but they know without doubt that in order to achieve it, they will have to work hard to catch up or modify their view of the American Dream a bit.

As with workers of any age, Gen Y employees want a supervisor who will respect and support them with kindness, good leadership, and flexibility. Adequate training and a platform for building success, coupled with positive and constructive criticism, are essential. Mentorship aimed at getting them ready to take on greater responsibility and enter management roles is also key in helping this generation Millennial succeed.

A few suggested daily reminders for Gen Y employees in the workplace:

- **You are changing the workplace, and it makes many people nervous. It is your opportunity.** Remember that most everyone, including your boss, will be viewing you and interacting with you from biases and expectations he or she would place upon others, for whatever reason. This may not be fair, but many studies show that it exists. In spite of the stereotypes, your generation has already made changes that are lasting as customers and as employees. Be aware of this possibility in your interactions with others, and keep those biases from impeding the success you're after.

- **You can build the career you want.** You know by now what it will take to reach your goals, and there is no time like the present to prove yourself where you are now or to seek a role better suited to your overall goals.

- **Careers are journeys and setbacks can provide valuable growth and lessons for you.** In many cases, your first few jobs may not be career material. However, there is something to be learned at every job, so do your best at each stop. If you've made mistakes, the best response is to learn and grow from them. With your hard work ethic and willingness to take chances when opportunities come along, you'll be highly qualified to step into your ideal position when it presents itself.

- **Position yourself for the role and career you want.** Continue to pursue the knowledge and training you need in order to be successful in your role, and find ways to contribute to the success of the organization. If you continue to do your best and you won't have regrets that may impact your success later. If you have intentions to stay with your employer, it will be important to have a plan for short-term and long-term success. In most cases, it will be up to you to make that plan. Seek help from experienced coworkers, your human resources department, or a mentor.

- **It is OK if you don't know what you want to be when you grow up.** The best advice I received in my late twenties was to be open to opportunities. Make sure your plan and your network allow for opportunities to come your way that can take you places you may not have even dreamed of yet. Be sure to review your career plan periodically so that you can measure your progress. Stay in touch with professionals and others whose opinions you value who can guide you and help you view your questions and concerns through different lenses. Whatever you do, don't give up.

Suggested Actions for Gen Y to Take

- **Remember your priorities.** You value both the compensation for your work and the time invested with family and friends. Unfortunately, it will mean that you must make trade-offs and be thoughtful in how you manage your life so that one choice doesn't come at the expense of the other. Take a little time to remember what is important to you and find ways to come to terms with trade-offs that you find acceptable.

- **Invest in your future.** Baby Boomers are leaving the workforce and Gen X alone cannot handle the void that remains. Invest in education and training and pursue visible success so that you will be first in line as your organization looks to your generation to step up.

- **Build and maintain your support system.** Ask the successful people you admire if they had mentors or role models coming up over the years. Chances are good that their answer will be an un-qualified "Yes." Your support system should include those like-minded friends and family members you can vent to, but also industry professionals and other highly successful individuals who will challenge you and tell you the truth, rather than just tell you things are great. Some of your network will come and go, and some will be with you forever. It will be important that you stay connected and proactively manage the relationships.

- **Have a contingency plan.** As you know from experience in down markets and with periods of job scarcity, nothing is guaranteed, even when you do everything right. Do your best to establish solid plans to save money for your future. If necessary, trim down your current lifestyle in order to do so. So expect to have three to six months of your living expenses in savings.

A Few Suggested Daily Reminders for Supervisors of Gen Y in the Workplace:

Remember that your Gen Y employee is just now solidly settled into his or her career, wise in some ways and still inexperienced in others. Most of your workers will soon be Millennial and Gen Z. Remember that these younger employees will wield a lot of influence in the coming decades. Viewing them as valued team members will make it easier to welcome their contributions.

- **The workplace has evolved. It's not necessarily wrong, it's just different. Keep an open mind.** Try to view Millennial ideas you may be uncomfortable with as just that—different—and not as bad or willful disagreement. Find common ground for difficult conversations and let them teach you something new.

- **Be a coach and model good leadership practices.** Encourage and model positive approaches on what it takes to succeed. Offer constructive criticism and pointers for success. Gen Y is watching and they strongly expect that you will be a boss they can look up to and respect.

- **Expect good things to happen. Be patient.** Being open to new ideas can propel your division to greater productivity or even toward a true breakthrough. It may take more conversation and a false start or two, but perseverance will pay off in the end.

Practical Suggestions for Supervisors of Millennials/Gen Y

☐ **Adjust your expectations.** Millennials are concerned about doing well in their roles and receiving appropriate feedback and compensation, so continue to relate to them on this level. However, they are also concerned with the bigger picture, which includes cultural issues as they impact the workplace, racially charged situations, ethical corporate behavior, and social connection, for example. Technology will also figure into the changes Millennials want to see happen. If you can move proactively in your organization to recognize and embrace these realities, potential upheaval due to misaligned employee expectations can be minimized and positive results realized sooner.

☐ **Communicate more.** Discussions about daily business issues will never go away, but Millennials will prefer more transparency at the table than you may be accustomed to sharing. They will request feedback as to their work performance, but they also want very clear guidance as to what it takes to get ahead and how progress is compensated. They need to see that their work is indeed tied to expected results, and will likely ask questions that may seem unrelated to you, but which have import for them.

❐ **Build good relationships. Relationship matter.** Millennials are more likely to view you, their supervisor, as an equal, and as a coach and be less concerned about protocols and more comfortable with sharing opinion. Work is a team effort, not a top down type approach. Your Gen Y employee will also be interested in your personal life, because work/life balance is important to them and it includes family and free-time interests.

Finally

Gen Y is highly educated, well grounded, and already aware of the impact that they will be making on the labor force over the next few decades. In spite of a rough start for many, most members of Gen Y are positive in terms of their own success and attainment of their version of the American Dream. They have experienced and witnessed the impact of the economic bust on Baby Boomer and Gen X family members, so they are realistic, practical, and appropriately cautious, but unwilling to lie down and give up.

The Millennial generation believes that great accomplishments and change are inevitable. They are equipped with innovative technology, quick access to information about virtually anything they want to know, and the diverse perspectives of their peers. With the guiding principles of justice, tolerance, ethical behavior, and a central place for family and friends, the hallmark of this generation will be the transfiguration of the American workplace as we know it now.

While it will take time for commonly held negative opinions to subside, my research did much to belie common attitudes that reinforce negative perceptions about Millennials; instead, it revealed a great Millennial sense of responsibility and self-direction that, if harnessed well, will indeed make the workplace a better place for generations to come.

Millennial/Gen Y Action Plan

Exercise 1
Preparing for Success

List the questions you will ask your supervisor about what success in your current role looks like and how you can best position yourself for raises and promotions.

1.

2.

3.

Who can you practice with to help you have a productive conversation?

- Mentor?
- Parent?
- Friend?

Exercise 2
Setting Priorities

List the top three things that will be important for you—
personally and/or professionally—in the next six to 12
months.

1.

2.

3.

Have at least two conversations with someone you trust
about how you accomplish these goals. Who will you ask?

1.

2.

Are you having trouble making a decision?

Sometimes a pros and cons list may not be enough—especially when you may place a higher value on certain aspects of your job or career. Try the following exercise that requires you to prioritize and weigh your options.

Directions:
1. List your choices in the choice columns.
2. List the key decision factors as a list in the left column.
3. If a key factor is very important, give it an importance multiplier. For example, if commute time is most important, you may want to give it a multiplier effect of 10. Give the best role a score of "1" and the least a score of "0." If they are the same, both get a "1" score.
4. Tally your score.
5. The highest score will help you decide your top priorities and serve as a starting point for your discussion or negotiation.
6. Once completed, discuss the results with someone you trust.

Decision: Example - Deciding to leave a job.

	Importance Multiplier (IM)	Choice One: Current Job		Choice Two: New Job	
	(Score: 1-10)	Score	Score with IM	Score	Score with IM
Short Commute	10	0	0	1	10
Pay Increase	5	0	0	1	5
Growth	5	0	0	1	5
Perks	0	1	0	1	0
Good Manager	10	1	10	0	0
Benefits	10	1	10	0	0
Company Culture	5	0	0	1	5
New Challenge	5	0	0	1	5
Stability	5	1	5	1	5
Travel	-10	0	0	1	-10
Scope of Role	2	1	2	1	2
New Skill Set	0	1	0	1	0
Mission	2	1	2	0	0
Total:		*5*	*28*	*11*	*27*

Decision: Example - Deciding to leave a job.

	Importance Multiplier (IM)	Choice One: Current Job		Choice Two: New Job	
	(Score: 1-10)	Score	Score with IM	Score	Score with IM
Total		5	28	11	27

In this example, if all things were equal, moving to the new job seems like an easy decision with a score of "11." However, when factors such as travel, benefits, and mission come into play, the decision to stay in your current role with a multiplier score of "28" may win out and lead you to engage in a bit more thought about what really matters at this point.

Are you having trouble making a decision?
Are you having trouble making a decision?

Sometimes a pros and cons list may not be enough—especially when you may place a higher value on certain aspects of your job or career. Try the following exercise that requires you to prioritize and weigh your options.

Directions:
1. List your choices in the choice columns.
2. List the key factors as a list in the left column,
3. If a key factor is very important, give it an importance multiplier. For example, if commute time is most important, you may want to give it a multiplier effect of 10. Give the best role a score of "1" and the least a score of "0." If they are the same, both get a "1" score.
4. Tally your score.
5. The highest score will help you decide your top priorities and serve as a starting point for your discussion or negotiation.
6. Once completed, discuss the results with someone you trust.

Decision:

	Importance Multiplier (IM)	Choice One: Current Job		Choice Two: New Job	
	(Score: 1-10)	Score	Score with IM	Score	Score with IM
Total:					

Exercise 3
Finding Success on the Job

Part 1: Be clear about what you want in your career right now. List the top three considerations you had in mind when you accepted the job offer with your current employer. Note whether those ideas are still important or if your thoughts have changed.

1.

2.

3.

Part 2: Put your thoughts into action. Now ask yourself what you can do to help create any change you want, and if you can stay if things don't change. Have a conversation about your thoughts with someone your trust.

1.

2.

3.

Part 3. Be intentional about managing your reputation.

1. What do you think that you are good at doing?

2. Ask at least five people what are you known for being good at doing.

3. What is your passion?

4. What are your values?

5. Invest in objective measures of your competencies. Take an assessment to understand your strengths and areas for development. Examples include: DISC, Myers-Briggs, and Strength Finders.

6. What is your level of engagement at work beyond your job?
   - Do you participate in social or after-work activities?
   - Do you volunteer for or are you asked to do special projects?
   - Do you deliver on your commitments?

7. What is your level of engagement in your chosen profession? Do you stay current in developments in your field? Do you belong to and/or are you active in professional organizations that relate to your industry?

8. Are you careful and thoughtful about your social and online presence? Have you performed an online search of your name? Are you
comfortable with what you found?

9. Summarize questions 1-8 into one paragraph. Refine the paragraph until you are comfortable that it reflects who you are and who
you want to be known as by others. Summarize the paragraph into
one sentence. Ask someone you trust if the statement you wrote
rings true. Use this as your guidepost.

10. Review this list at least once a year.
  • Find an accountability partner to keep you focused.
  • Refine and revise as needed.

Exercise 4
Building a Support Network

Think of two people within your organization who you admire and could help you discover and plan your career trajectory. One of those people could be your boss; another could be another employee who's been with the company for a long time.

Arrange to have a conversation with them during a time that does not interfere with your (or their) work responsibilities. Tell them you'd like to share what you admire about them and what they do, and ask them if they would be open to helping you to learn more.

Remember to follow up and to thank them for their help. If they decline your request, still be polite and find someone else to ask.

Who will you ask, and when will you ask?

What will you share about your goals and plans?

What next steps will you take?

Exercise 5
Creating a Career Reassessment Map

As you build your career, it's often helpful to step back and assess whether you're where you thought you'd be. Complete the chart below and then ask for input from someone you trust.

1. Define the role and skills where you are now. List the skills used for your current role.

Current Role: Retail Associate

Skills Needed: working with customers, communication skills, time management, cashier experience, team player, flexibility

Current Role:

Skills Needed:

2. Identify the next roles you're interested in pursuing and list the skills you'll need for them. Examples can be found by searching employment websites or by talking to someone already in that role.

Next Role: Manager

Skills Needed: hire and develop staff, budget management, maintain employee work schedules, prepare reports, agility, interpersonal skills

Next Role:

Skills Needed:

3. Identify the training and/or education needed for your next role. Examples can be found by searching job descriptions or by talking to someone already in that role.

Next Role: Manager

Training/Education Needed: Bachelor's degree or equivalent

Next Role:

Training/Education Needed:

4. Identify the gaps in your background and training with the role you are seeking. Review the job description against your own experience and training to identify abilities you already have that you can transfer, or the skills you need to acquire. Note: it does not have to match 100%. List the areas where you need to gain more experience.

5. Create a plan to fill the gap. Think about ways that you can learn more about what the job entails and how you can get the experience and training you need. Talk with someone already in the role, or someone who supervises that role.

Example: Information interview with a manager at your organization, join a professional group, serve as a team leader or project leader to gain experience leading others, or speak with someone to help you brainstorm ideas about how to build out your next steps.

Who will you contact?

6. Make a plan with appropriate dates and milestones for attaining the skills for your next role, and find someone to keep you accountable and encourage you.

Checklist for Supervisors

☐ **The workplace has evolved. It's not necessarily wrong; it's just different.** Try to view the Millennial ideas you may be uncomfortable with as just that—different—and not as bad or willful disagreement. Find common ground for difficult conversations and let them teach you something new.

☐ **Be a coach and model good leadership practices.** Encourage and model positive approaches on what it takes to succeed. Offer constructive criticism and pointers for success. Gen Y is watching and they strongly expect that you will be a boss they can look up to and respect.

☐ **Expect good things to happen.** Being open to new ideas can propel your division to greater productivity or even to a true breakthrough. It may take more conversation and a false start or two, but perseverance will pay off in the end.

☐ **Set them up for success.** Perhaps when you started your career, the expectations for employees were different than they are today. You might have entered the workplace with an in-depth training program or you might have been left to problem-solve on your own. Surviving a *trial by fire* experience isn't necessarily a badge of honor for Millennials. If they are frustrated and can't see a path toward sustained success, they may leave.

☐ **Encourage the practical aspects of career advancement and put the plan in place.** Due to the economy, many Millennials have had a delayed start to their careers and are now eager to catch up. Think of ways to reinforce good work habits and skills that will serve them well in any undertaking, not just in your department. Millennials have several years under their belt and have expectations about growing in their roles and careers.

☐ **Be transparent about compensation.** Financial security is important to your Millennial employee, and so they may be focused on advancement and bonuses. It will be important to have conversations about compensation in all forms (e.g., salary, bonuses, vacation, other benefits) to manage their expectations.

☐ **Recognize how they may be shaped by key personal and professional values.** From a personal perspective, *happiness* and *relationships* ranked highly for Gen Y. Professionally, Gen Y values *making more money* and *doing well in their current role*. As you think about the team atmosphere and your leadership style, consider how the quality of your interactions and the work experience will matter to your Millennial employees. Coaching them to excel on the job and being clear about their opportunities to earn more money will be key to retention.

☐ **Offer constructive feedback when it is warranted.** Generation Y is used to instant feedback for their ideas due to their frequent use of social media during their formative years. Give them what they need to fully perform what you're asking of them, including encouraging words. Be thoughtful about requests for better or different work, and make sure you also share truthful assurances regarding what you appreciate about their work.

☐ **Be clear about their options.** Be sure to let them know they are valued in their current role and be willing to be open and realistic about their career prospects. Whether you are presenting job options within your team or laterally within your organization, encourage your employees to explore and do what they can to position themselves for moving on if they have mastered their current position. Coach them to move sideways when you can, and be supportive of their choices to move on if they do.

☐ **Support family and work-life balance.** Allow flexibility with work schedules. Relationships and happiness are extremely important to your Millennial workers, so be careful to not treat these as afterthoughts in your interactions with your team members. Gen Y-ers who feel that you value what they value will be more satisfied and more likely to go the extra mile for you.

☐ **Create a platform for problem-solving.** Make time to listen to your Millennials and get their ideas about what's going on with the department and the company. Answer their hard questions as best you can and address their complaints and concerns. Keep an open mind as you solicit their input.

☐ **Create an ideal work setting.** The work environment matters to Millennials. Whether it is the tone you set or the culture at your office, this generation isn't comfortable with a cold or sterile setting with a "punch the clock" and "heads down" style. They tend to see work as an extension of their lives. Flexibility in approach, location, hours, and atmosphere all make a difference in productivity, tenure, and loyalty.

☐ **Be generous with constructive feedback.** Remind yourself that your Gen Y worker is used to all sorts of input with which to evaluate and make decisions, and the most user-friendly resources will win out. Make professional feedback, company information, and appropriate training readily available. Plan ways to gather their ideas and utilize their preferences to make the workplace and work process as attractive and satisfactory as possible.

❏ **Provide training.** For many Millennials, the path to an ideal role was a journey. Now that they've arrived, they want to do well. Training is an investment in your employees and sets them up for success. The training can be done by you, via courses that your company provides or external sources. Don't wait for them to ask for training; consider making the investment in job skills and professional development to set them up for success.

❏ **Capitalize on their strengths.** Are you using each employee to their fullest? Try to arrange tasks and systems to utilize your Gen Y worker's skills to their fullest, adding challenges as well. Solicit their ideas as to how to improve processes and make them responsible for implementing the change.

❏ **Be mindful that all your actions matter.** Command and control styles don't appear to play well with Gen Y. Employees pay close attention to how you conduct yourself. Your behavior and leadership will shape the future of your company and the workplace. A respectful and supportive supervisor will bring out your Gen Y workers' best efforts, and they can become your best long-term assets.

❏ **Share constructive feedback.** Lead Gen Y in continuing to develop a strong life-long work ethic by setting clear expectations and offering incentives and examples. Specific feedback and judicious correction are helpful, after you take the time to listen and understand where your younger workers are coming from.

❏ **Respect rules the day.** Gen Y is responsive to respectful, as-equals interaction, not inflexible command-and-control methods. They want to contribute meaningfully and be recognized for the value they add, but if they are demeaned or unheard, they will be less willing to respond well to what you're saying.

❐ **Accept that the workplace is an extension of their lives.** It is more than just a job. Expect to have to address things other than the work process. More and more employees find workplace culture to be as important, if not more important, than the work they do and the compensation they receive. Even if this seems irrelevant to you, remember that your Gen Y employees will look elsewhere if too much is unattractive about their whole work experience.

❐ **Adjust your expectations.** Millennials are concerned about doing well in their roles and receiving appropriate feedback and compensation, so continue to relate to them on this level. However, they are also concerned with the bigger picture, which includes cultural issues as they impact the workplace, racially charged situations, ethical corporate behavior, and social connection, for example. Technology will also figure into the changes Millennials want to see happen. If you can move proactively in your organization to recognize and embrace these realities, potential upheaval due to misaligned employee expectations can be minimized and positive results realized sooner.

❐ **Communicate more.** Discussions about daily business issues will never go away, but Millennials will prefer more transparency at the table than you may be accustomed to sharing. They will request feedback as to their work performance, but they also want very clear guidance as to what it takes to get ahead and how progress is compensated. They need to see that their work is indeed tied to expected results, and will likely ask questions that may seem unrelated to you, but which have import for them.

❐ **Build good relationships. Relationships matter.** Millennials are more likely to view you, their supervisor, as an equal, and as a coach and be less concerned about protocols and more comfortable with sharing opinion. Work is a team effort, not a top down type approach. Your Gen Y employee will also be interested in your personal life, because work/life balance is important to them and it includes family and free-time interests.

ABOUT THE GENERATIONS IN THE WORKPLACE SERIES

This book series is based on the findings of a study that was conducted in the fall of 2016, to identify what is important to employees in the multigenerational workplace. The goal of the series is to provide practical advice to professionals as they navigate their careers and to serve as a resource for managers and coworkers within age-diverse workforces.

About 1,000 U.S. citizens born between 1946 and 1998 responded to a survey that was professionally facilitated by an independent research organization. The final validated sample for this study included nearly 700 employed individuals who were college graduates (Baby Boomers, Gen Z, and Gen Y) and employed college students (Gen Z). The gender makeup in the sample was split 50/50 male/female. Twenty-three percent of the sample were members of Generation Y.

The study included a 35-question multiple-choice survey in which the respondents were asked to select the best answer, rank a series of concepts, or write in a response to certain questions. I also conducted interviews with members of Gen Y. The core questions I wanted to explore were:

- What values are foundational to each generation's motivations?
- How do the respondents feel about their career as well as their personal and professional values?
- How do employees of each generation perceive and interact with those of other generations?
- What does each generation want from their supervisor to make them more successful in their role?

Most specifically, I wanted to explore the factors that help people succeed in their careers, and to determine how individuals and organizations achieve goals in multigenerational workplaces.

After reviewing several previous studies on the generational cohorts, I chose these birth years to represent the groups identified in the research for this book:

- Baby Boomer 1946–1964: ages 52–70*
- Gen X 1965–1980: ages 36–51
- Gen Y (Millennials) 1981–1995: ages 21–35
- Gen Z born after 1995: ages 20 and under**

* Age at the time of the study
** The study included only 18- to 20-year-old participants

REFERENCES

1. Press release. (2015, June 15). Millennials outnumber baby boomers and are far more diverse, Census Bureau reports. United States Census Bureau. Retrieved 05/16/2016 from https://www.census.gov/newsroom/press-releases/2015/cb15-113.html

2. Pew Research Center. (2015, May 11). Millennials surpass Gen Xers as the largest generation in the U.S. labor force. Pew Research Center. Retrieved 05/17/2017 from http://www.pewresearch.org/fact-tank/2015/05/11/millennials-surpass-gen-xers-as-the-largest-generation-in-u-s-labor-force/

3. O'Malley, B. (2016, April 25). Millennials and 'Their Destruction of Civilization.' Forbes. Retrieved 05/17/2017 from https://www.forbes.com/sites/valleyvoices/2016/04/25/millennials-and-their-destruction-of-civilization/#37a3c5b32830

4. Shah, R. (2011, April 20). Working with five generations in the workplace. Forbes. Retrieved 05/17/2017 from https://www.forbes.com/sites/rawnshah/2011/04/20/working-with-five-generations-in-the-workplace/#25d5e5123e7a

5. Sharf, S. (2015, August 24). What is a 'Millennial' anyway? Meet the man who coined the phrase. Forbes. Retrieved 05/17/2017 from https://www.forbes.com/sites/samanthasharf/2015/08/24/what-is-a-millennial-anyway-meet-the-man-who-coined-the-phrase/#25c3d8cf4a05

6. Schwarz, H. (2015, May 15). Millennials: The generation that 66 percent of millennials would rather not associate with. The Washington Post. Retrieved 05/17/2017 from https://www.washingtonpost.com/news/the-fix/wp/2015/05/15/millennials-the-generation-

that-even-millennials-would-rather-not-associate-
with/?utm_term=.8e57a77055fc

7. Pew Research Center. (February, 2010). Millennials: A portrait of
generation next. Confident. Connected. Open to Change. Pew Research Center. Retrieved 05/17/2017 from http://assets.pewre-
search.org/wp-content/uploads/sites/3/2010/10/millennials-confident-
connected-open-to-change.pdf

8. Fleming, J. (2016, May 19). Gallup analysis: Millennials, marriage
and family. Gallup. Retrieved 05/17/2017 from http://www.gal-
lup.com/poll/191462/gallup-analysis-millennials-marriage-fam-
ily.aspx

9. *Ibid.*

10. Kroll, T., Murphy, S. (2012, July 27). The events that have shaped
the Millennial era. American Enterprise Institute. Retrieved 5/17/2017
from http://www.aei.org/publication/the-events-that-have-shaped-
the-millennial-era

11. Mayhew, R. (2017). How is technology impacting the changes in
the 21st century workplace? Chron. Retrieved 05/17/2017 from
http://smallbusiness.chron.com/technology-impacting-changes-21st-
century-workplace-3357.html

12. Chaney, P. (2016, July 25). 20 Surprising stats about the gig economy. Small Business Trends. Retrieved 05/17/2017 from
https://smallbiztrends.com/2016/07/20-surprising-stats-freelance-econ-
omy.html

13. Blog post. (2017). 5 American hiring trends to watch in 2017. Un-
dercover Recruiter. Retrieved 05/17/2017 from http://theundercoverre-
cruiter.com/hiring-trends-watch/

14. DeZube, D. (2017). Bye bye boomers: Who will fill your workforce gap? Monster. Retrieved 05/17/2017 from https://hiring.mon-ster.com/hr/hr-best-practices/recruiting-hiring-advice/strategic-work-force-planning/baby-boomer-workforce-gap.aspx

15. Gani, A. (2016, March 15). Millennials at work: Five stereotypes - and why they are (mostly) wrong. The Guardian (U.S. edition). Re-trieved 05/17/2017 from https://www.theguard-ian.com/world/2016/mar/15/millennials-work-five-stereotypes-generation-y-jobs

16. Singh, S. (2014. May 14). The 10 social and tech trends that could shape the next decade. Forbes. Retrieved 05/17/2017 from https://www.forbes.com/sites/sarwantsingh/2014/05/12/the-top-10-mega-trends-of-the-decade/#3e0727f6a62c

17. Study report. (2015, November 5). Green generation: Millennials say sustainability is a shopping priority. Nielsen. Retrieved 05/17/2017 from http://www.nielsen.com/us/en/insights/news/2015/green-genera-tion-millennials-say-sustainability-is-a-shopping-priority.html

18. Lachman, M.L., Brett, D. (2015, May). Gen Y and housing: What they want and where they want it. Urban Land Institute. Retrieved 05/17/2017 from http://americas.uli.org/wp-content/up-loads/sites/125/ULI-Documents/Gen-Y-and-Housing.pdf

19. 18. Mullins, L. (2010, February 1). The future of housing demand: 4 key demographic trends. U.S. News & World Report. Retrieved 05/17/2017 from http://money.usnews.com/money/personal-fi-nance/real-estate/articles/2010/02/01/the-future-of-housing-demand-4-key-demographic-trends

20. Steinberg, S. (2016, April 19). Futurist speaker: Generation Y and Gen Z trends. A Keynote Speaker. Retrieved 05/17/2017 from

http://akeynotespeaker.com/futurist-speaker-generation-y-millenni-als-trends/

21. Frey, W. H. (2016, June 28). Diversity defines the millennial gener-ation. Brookings. Retrieved 05/17/2017 from https://www.brook-ings.edu/blog/the-avenue/2016/06/28/diversity-defines-the-millennial-generation/

22. *Ibid.*

23. Mayhew, R. (2017), How is technology impacting the changes, *supra*.

24. Twenge, J.M. (2016, November 16). Five reasons why millennials helped elect Donald Trump. Psychology Today. Retrieved 0/17/2017 from https://www.psychologytoday.com/blog/our-changing-cul-ture/201611/five-reasons-why-millennials-helped-elect-donald-trump

25. Blake, A. (2016 December 2). Yes, you can blame Millennials for Hillary Clinton's loss. The Washington Post. Retrieved 05/17/2017 from https://www.washingtonpost.com/news/the-fix/wp/2016/12/02/yes-you-can-blame-millennials-for-hillary-clintons-loss/?utm_term=.6d3bb3c49708

26. Eccles, J. S., & Wigfield, A. (2002, February). Motivational Beliefs, Values, and Goals. Annual Review of Psychology, 53(1), 109–132. Re-trieved 05/17/2017 from https://doi.org/10.1146/an-nurev.psych.53.100901.135153

27. Lerman, K., (2015). How Millennials are reshaping health and wellness. C Space Reports. Retrieved 05/172017 from http://cdn2.hub-spot.net/hubfs/373439/C_Space_Reports/Millenni-alHealthCare_Ebook_F_3_REBRAND.pdf?t=1491846128792

28. Study report. (2016). Winning over the next generation of leaders. Deloitte. Retrieved 05/17/2017 from https://www2.deloitte.com/content/dam/Deloitte/global/Documents/About-Deloitte/gx-millenial-survey-2016-exec-summary.pdf

29. Landrum, S. (2017, January 9). How Millennials' happiness is tied to work friendships. Forbes. Retrieved 05/17/2017 from https://www.forbes.com/sites/sarahlandrum/2017/01/09/how-millennials-happiness-is-tied-to-work-friendships/#3e4a362c133d

30. Kolowich, L. (2015, January 8). 11 Reasons having friends at work makes you happier. Hubspot infographic. Retrieved 05/17/2017 from https://blog.hubspot.com/marketing/workplace-friendships#sm.0000ybv1ghqtodvzriq1tl7cn8xxf

31. Kollmeyer, B. (2016, April 5). When it comes to saving money, millennials are killing it. Market Watch. Retrieved 05/17/2017 from http://www.marketwatch.com/story/when-it-comes-to-saving-money-millennials-are-killing-it-2016-03-30

32. Rampton, J. (2017, February 3). This is how Millennials are saving money. Mashable. Retrieved 05/17/2017 from http://mashable.com/2017/02/03/how-millennials-are-saving-money/#BejztmqwuPqr

33. Adams, J. T. (1931). The Epic of America, Boston, MA: Little, Brown & Company.

34. Survey report. (2015, November). Survey of young Americans' attitudes toward politics and public service, 28th Edition. Harvard University Institute of Politics. Retrieved 05/17/2017 from http://iop.harvard.edu/sites/default/files_new/pictures/151208_Harvard_IOP_Fall_2015_Topline.pdf

35. Chew, J. (2015, December 11). Half of Millennials believe the American dream is dead. Fortune. Retrieved 05/17/2017 from http://fortune.com/2015/12/11/american-dream-millennials-dead/

36. Averna, M. (2016, January 27). The higher education trap: Why millennials can't win when it comes to a college education. GenFKD. Retrieved 05/17/2017 from http://www.genfkd.org/higher-education-trap-why-millennials-cant-win-college

37. *Ibid.*

38. Lyubomirsky, S., King, L., Diener, E. (2005) The benefits of frequent positive affect: Does happiness lead to success? American Psychological Association Journal Bulletin Vol. 131, No. 6, 803–855. Retrieved 05/17/2017 from http://www.apa.org/pubs/journals/releases/bul-1316803.pdf

39. Press release. (2016, June 24). American time use survey summary. U.S. Department of Labor. Retrieved 05/17/2017 from http://www.bls.gov/news.release/atus.nr0.htm

40. Key findings. (2013, July 15). 2013 U.S. Workplace study. Gensler. Retrieved from http://www.gensler.com/research-insight/research/the-2013-us-workplace-survey-1?q=us%20workplace%20survey

41. Wobbrock, J. (2014). How Millennials require us to design the technologies of tomorrow. Wired. Retrieved 05/17/2017 from https://www.wired.com/insights/2014/09/millennials-design-technologies/

42. May, J. (2016, July 31). Millennials and technology drive the innovation train. The Tennessean. Retrieved 05/17/2017 from http://www.tennessean.com/story/money/tech/2016/07/31/millennials-and-technology-drive-innovation-train/87748698/

43. Duke, B. (2016, March 3). When I was your age. Center for American Progress. Retrieved 0/17/2017 from https://www.americanprogress.org/issues/economy/reports/2016/03/03/131627/when-i-was-your-age/

44. *Ibid.*

45. Study report. (2017 January). Financial health of young America: Measuring generational declines between Baby Boomers & Millennials. Young Invincibles. Retrieved 05/17/2017 from http://younginvincibles.org/wp-content/uploads/2017/01/FHYA-Final2017-1.pdf

46. Study fact sheet. (2016). Evaluate a job offer study. Fidelity Investments. Retrieved 05/17/2017 from https://www.fidelity.com/bin-public/060_www_fidelity_com/documents/fidelity-job-offer-fact-sheet.pdf

47. Infographic. (2016). Millennials@Work: Perspectives on diversity & inclusion. Weber Shandwick. Retrieved 05/17/2017 from http://www.webershandwick.com/news/article/millennials-at-work-perspectives-on-diversity-inclusion

48 Press release. (2015, June 15), Note 1, *supra.*

49. Yazykova, E. McLeigh, J.D., (2015, September). Millennial children of immigrant parents: Transnationalism, disparities, policy, and potential. American Journal of Orthopsychiatry 85(5S):S38-44. doi: 10.1037/ort0000114. Retrieved 05/17/2017 from https://www.ncbi.nlm.nih.gov/pubmed/26460713

50. Pew Research Center. (2016, October 6). The state of American jobs. Pew Research Center. Retrieved 05/17/2017 from http://www.pewsocialtrends.org/2016/10/06/the-state-of-american-jobs/

51. *Ibid.*

52. Pew Research Center. (February, 2010), *supra*.

53. Pew Research Center. (2014, March 7). Millennials in adulthood. Pew Social Trends. Retrieved 05/172017 from http://www.pewsocial-trends.org/2014/03/07/millennials-in-adulthood/

54. Pew Research Center. (2015, March 17). Millennials on track to be the most educated generation to date. Pew Research Center. Retrieved 05/17/2017 from http://www.pewresearch.org/fact-tank/2015/03/19/how-millennials-compare-with-their-grandparents/ft_millennials-education_031715/

55. Pew Research Center. (2014, February 11). The rising cost of not going to college. Pew Social Trends. Retrieved 05/17/2017 from http://www.pewsocialtrends.org/2014/02/11/the-rising-cost-of-not-going-to-college/

56. Study report. (2016). Job seeker nation study: Where job seekers stand on the economy, job security, and the future of work. Jobvite. Retrieved 05/17/2017 from http://www.jobvite.com/wp-content/uploads/2016/03/Jobvite_Jobseeker_Nation_2016.pdf

57. Amabile, T. M., Conti, R., Coon, H., Lazenby, J., and Herron, M. (1996, October). Assessing the work environment for creativity. Academy of Management Journal 39, no. 5. Retrieved 05/17/2017 from http://people.wku.edu/richard.miller/amabile.pdf

58. Asghar, R. (2014, January 13). What Millennials want in the workplace (And why you should start giving it to them). Forbes. Retrieved 05/17/2017 from https://www.forbes.com/sites/robasghar/2014/01/13/what-millennials-want-in-the-workplace-and-why-you-should-start-giving-it-to-them/#4815b9254c4

59. George, D., Whitehouse, C., Whitehouse, P. (2011). A model of intergenerativity: how the intergenerational school is bringing the generations together to foster collective wisdom and community health. Journal of Intergenerational Relationships, 9:4, 389-404. Retrieved from https://www.healthandenvironment.org/docs/WhitehouseA_Model_of_Intergenerativity.pdf

ABOUT THE AUTHOR

Dr. Candace Steele Flippin lives by the philosophy that bringing multiple perspectives to the table results in better outcomes. She is an inspiring speaker and highly regarded executive. As an award-winning public affairs leader, she has worked at Fortune 500 companies, a global public relations agency, and national non-profit organizations. She is also a Research Fellow at the Weatherhead School of Management at Case Western Reserve University, where she researches the multigenerational workplace.

Books by Dr. Candace Steele Flippin:

Generation Z in the Workplace: Helping the Newest Generation in the Workforce Build Successful Working Relationships and Career Paths

Millennials in the Workplace: Helping the Largest Generation Group Succeed at Work and in Their Careers

Available on Kindle and in Paperback on Amazon

Connect with her at www.CandaceSteeleFlippin.com

Made in the USA
San Bernardino, CA
22 July 2017